My Name Is Funky... and I'm an Alcoholic

A Story about Alcoholism and Recovery

From the Celebrated Comic Strip *Funky Winkerbean*

Syndicated in More Than 400 Newspapers Nationwide

■   ■   ■

By Tom Batiuk

HAZELDEN

Hazelden

Center City, Minnesota 55012-0176

1-800-328-0094

1-651-213-4590 (Fax)

www.hazelden.org

Funky Winkerbean comic strip content © 2007 by Batom, Inc.

Resource section © 2007 by Hazelden

ISBN: 978-1-59285-377-9

Library of Congress Cataloging-in-Publication Data

Batiuk, Tom.
   My name is Funky- and I'm an alcoholic : a story about
alcoholism and recovery / by Tom Batiuk.
      p. cm.
   ISBN 978-1-59285-377-9 (softcover)
   1. Alcoholics-Comic books, strips, etc.   2. Alcoholics-
Rehabilitation-Comic books, strips, etc.   3. Alcoholics
Anonymous-Comic books, strips, etc.   4. Twelve step
programs-Comic books, strips, etc.   I. Title.
      HV5275.B394 2007
      616.86'1-dc22

                                            2007011199

11   10   09   08   07   1   2   3   4   5   6

Cover design by Tom Batiuk and David Spohn

Interior design and typesetting by Prism Publishing Center

To the Arid Fellowship

Acknowledgments

Comic strips are not produced in a vacuum, and the work contained herein is no exception. I'd like to acknowledge the following people whose contributions helped make this collection what it is. Thanks to Chuck Ayers, Lee Loughridge, Bill Sandor, and the gang at King Features for helping me take Funky to new places.

I'd also like to thank the folks at the Arid Fellowship for the kindness, generosity, and insights they provided for the stranger in their midst.

Finally, I'd like to thank my wife, Cathy, for her patience, understanding, and love, and for creating the space for this work to be brought into existence. We're going on that vacation now, Sweetie.

Introduction

The story of Funky's battle with alcohol was a long time in coming. Not only did my skills and abilities as an artist need to grow before I could properly tackle such a story arc, but my characters needed to mature as well.

Even with those elements in place, the hard work of telling this story was only beginning. It was daunting to test my eponymous lead character with something as potentially devastating as alcoholism. Nothing like this had ever been done before in comic strips. The approach to alcoholism in the comics has long mirrored the misconceptions of society. The depiction of problem drinking has typically been old school and can be traced to pratfalling drunks in vaudevillian sketches. Whether it was a hard-drinking army colonel, an unemployed, sponging ne'er-do-well, or a besotted court jester, the alcoholic's problems were always treated as the butt of the joke. Attention was never paid to the pain of the alcoholic and those around him or her.

It seemed to me that the comics were capable of more. As with all art, comic strips can be a venue to help order the world, to help the observer fill in the blanks for the insights or truth that may be missing. As an artist, I believe that I should challenge not only my expectations, but those of my audience as well. I also believe that comic strips can be thought provoking, rather than simply humorous. If I was going to tackle alcoholism, I wanted to cast aside the stereotypes and deal with the reality.

In order to do that, I needed to get the facts about the disease. My initial research started with a lot of reading, which, of course, led to Alcoholics Anonymous (AA). This was followed by a reading of *Twelve Steps and Twelve Traditions* and a visit to an AA meeting. Eventually, I stood on the front lawn of the house in Akron, Ohio, where AA founder Bill W. had lived. In fact, Bill W.'s house can be seen in the background as Funky and his sponsor, Wade, walk past it on a chilly winter's evening.

While technical facts are important, it's the human aspect that drives the story. Most human experience is understandable if you're willing to honestly look within for the emotions that drive us all. I tend to think of that process as a compassionate artifice that allows an artist to identify and empathize and tap into the core elements that define us as human. We all carry within us the seeds for growth, as well as the seeds for our own destruction.

Every work speaks to some audience. Taking the thought one step further, good art makes people believe the artist, and the best art makes them believe in themselves. My hope for this work is that it can be a beginning step in that latter direction.

Tom Batiuk

November 2006

Editor's Note

Since its 1972 debut, the strip *Funky Winkerbean* has developed an extensive cast of characters. For readers who are new to the story, here's a brief introduction to the main characters in *My Name Is Funky:*

Funky Winkerbean and his wife, **Cindy Summers,** met at Westview High School. Cindy is a high-powered television anchor. Funky worked at Montoni's Pizza during high school and today is a co-owner. The marriage between "the most popular girl and the guy with the goofiest name" was an unlikely one. Stress over careers and other issues is taking its toll.

Les Moore was Funky's best friend in high school. He is an English teacher and newspaper advisor at Westview. His wife, **Lisa,** is a fledgling attorney and works at Montoni's to help pay bills. The couple live in a storefront apartment above Montoni's.

Wally Winkerbean is Funky's nephew. One night on a date with his girl-friend **Becky,** he drove while drunk and totaled his car. Rescuers needed the jaws of life to save the couple, and Becky's arm was amputated as a result. Wally enlisted in the army to avoid the shame of seeing Becky. He is now serving in Iraq.

Wade was homeless when he was hired by Funky as Montoni's handyman.

Holly, who emerges later in *My Name Is Funky,* had a secret crush on Funky in high school. She and Lisa belong to a breast cancer survivor support group.

SO WHERE ARE YOU TWO OFF TO?

BATIUK
3-27

CINDY'S BEST FRIEND, CARRIE, FROM HIGH SCHOOL IS ABOUT TO TIE THE NOOSE... SO WE'RE GOING TO THE WEDDING DECEPTION!

YOU KNOW, IF SOMEONE TOLD YOU THAT YOU WERE WITTY... THEY LIED!

SO HOW ARE THINGS WITH YOU AND FUNKY?

3-28

OH... WE'VE GOT OUR UPS AND DOWNS...

MY CAREER IS GOING UP... AND IT'S REALLY GETTING HIM DOWN!

YOU KNOW, CARRIE... YOU'VE ALWAYS BEEN THERE FOR ME!

IF SOME GIRL WAS BUGGING ME BACK WHEN WE WERE IN HIGH SCHOOL... YOU'D SPREAD ENOUGH RUMORS ABOUT HER TO RUIN HER FOR THE REST OF HER HIGH SCHOOL CAREER!

BATIUK

YOU REALLY UNDERSTOOD THE TRUE MEANING OF FRIENDSHIP!

3-29

1

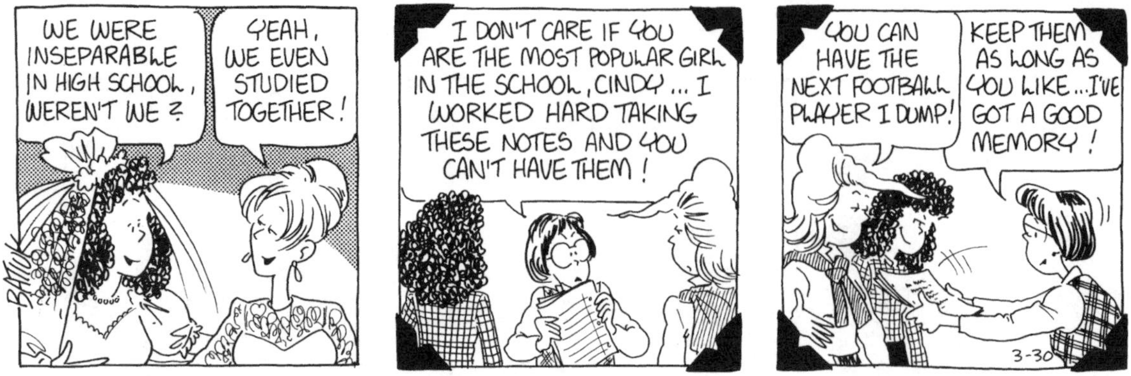
WE WERE INSEPARABLE IN HIGH SCHOOL, WEREN'T WE?
YEAH, WE EVEN STUDIED TOGETHER!
I DON'T CARE IF YOU ARE THE MOST POPULAR GIRL IN THE SCHOOL, CINDY... I WORKED HARD TAKING THESE NOTES AND YOU CAN'T HAVE THEM!
YOU CAN HAVE THE NEXT FOOTBALL PLAYER I DUMP!
KEEP THEM AS LONG AS YOU LIKE... I'VE GOT A GOOD MEMORY!
3-30

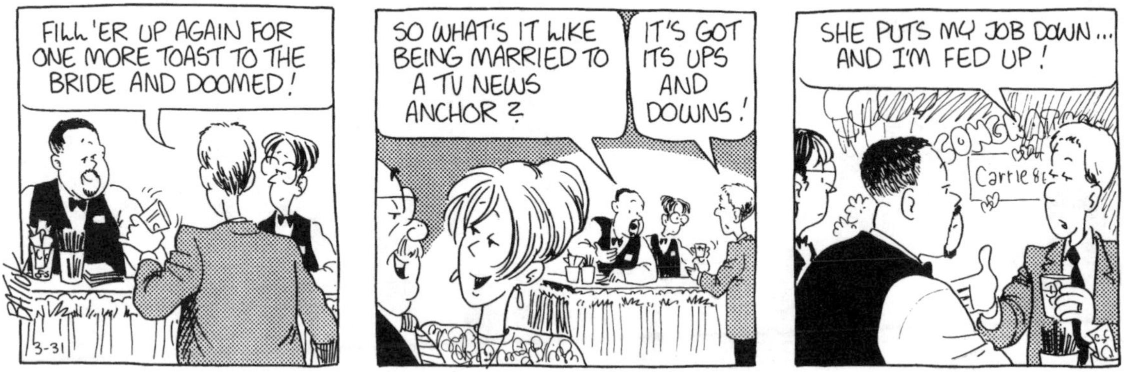
FILL 'ER UP AGAIN FOR ONE MORE TOAST TO THE BRIDE AND DOOMED!
3-31
SO WHAT'S IT LIKE BEING MARRIED TO A TV NEWS ANCHOR?
IT'S GOT ITS UPS AND DOWNS!
SHE PUTS MY JOB DOWN... AND I'M FED UP!

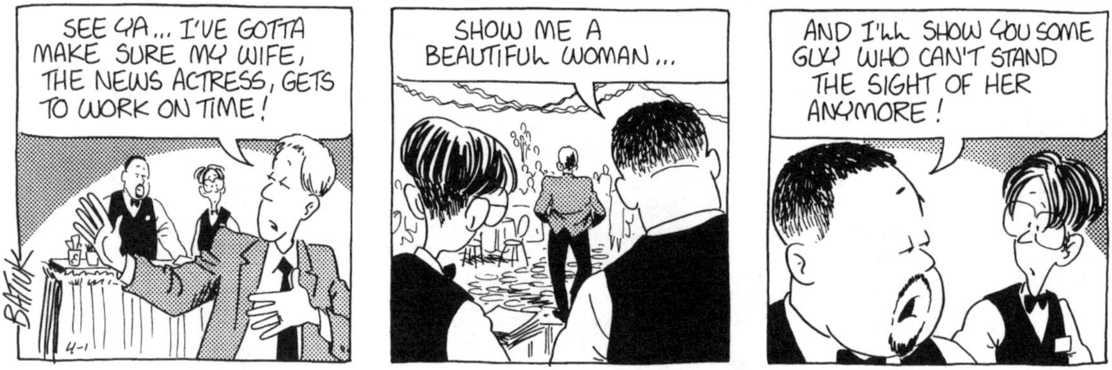
SEE YA... I'VE GOTTA MAKE SURE MY WIFE, THE NEWS ACTRESS, GETS TO WORK ON TIME!
4-1
SHOW ME A BEAUTIFUL WOMAN...
AND I'LL SHOW YOU SOME GUY WHO CAN'T STAND THE SIGHT OF HER ANYMORE!

NOW THAT SPRING IS HERE, TONY,... I THOUGHT WE COULD IMPROVE OUR LUNCHEON BUSINESS BY ADDING SOME CAFÉ-STYLE TABLES OUT HERE!

BUT WHY, FUNKY? THE BUSINESS HAS NEVER BEEN IN BETTER FINANCIAL SHAPE!

IF WE AIN'T BROKE... DON'T FIX US!

5-8

I STILL DON'T KNOW WHY WE HAVE TO EXPAND OUR BUSINESS, FUNKY!

WHERE'S THE PASSION, TONY? DON'T YOU REMEMBER WHAT IT WAS LIKE WHEN YOU WERE STARTING OUT AND YOU WERE LEAN, MEAN AND FULL OF FIRE?

MONTONI'S Pizza

ACTUALLY... I WAS LEAN AND MAINLY FULL OF FEAR!

5-9

THIS SIDEWALK KIND OF ATMOSPHERE CAN HELP SEPARATE US FROM THE BIG FRANCHISE OPERATIONS, TONY!

IT'S THE LAW OF THE COMMERCIAL JUNGLE...

DO LUNCH OR BE LUNCH!

MONTONI'S

5-10

THERE! EVERYTHING IS READY FOR ALFRESCO DINING!

5-11

AS CAPTAIN KIRK USED TO SAY... BRACE FOR IMPACT!

YOU WANT TO SERVE **HOT DOGS** AT LUNCH!?

5-12

CARLO IS A **CHEF!!** HE DOES NOT WARM UP **HOT DOGS!!**

I'D SAY FUNKY'S NEW LUNCHEON IDEAS ARE HAVING AN IMPACT ON OUR BUSINESS ALREADY!

I FINALLY CONVINCED CARLO TO COME BACK TO WORK AND THEN CINDY CALLS AND ASKS IF I CAN GIVE HER KID SISTER A JOB FOR THE SUMMER!

5-13

I'LL TELL YOU, LES... IT NEVER ENDS AROUND HERE!

DO YOU THINK THAT MAYBE YOU'RE PUSHING YOURSELF A LITTLE TOO HARD?

UNFORTUNATELY... THE WORLD DOESN'T GIVE ME MUCH OF A CHOICE!

SO HOW SOON CAN YOU START, SADIE?

ACTUALLY... I'D LIKE TO TAKE A COUPLE OF WEEKS AND JUST SORT OF VEG OUT BEFORE I GO TO WORK!

GEE... NORMALLY YOU GIVE TWO WEEKS NOTICE WHEN YOU'RE ABOUT TO QUIT A JOB!

5-15

SO CINDY'S KID SISTER IS GOING TO BE WORKING HERE OVER THE SUMMER?

YEP!

MONTONI'S IS REALLY GETTING TO BE A BUSTLING PLACE!

I KNOW... IF THIS WERE A COMIC STRIP, READERS WOULDN'T BE ABLE TO KEEP TRACK OF ALL THE CHARACTERS!

ISN'T IT A LITTLE EARLY IN THE DAY FOR THAT?

HEY... IT HELPS ME TO BE LIKE THE MUSHROOMS ON OUR PIZZAS...

5-17

A FUN-GUY!

OUCH! AND I THOUGHT I WAS BAD!

BOY... IT MUST BE PRETTY WINDY UP BY THE LAKE TODAY... CINDY'S HAIR ALMOST MOVED!

DID YOU HEAR WHAT FUNKY SAID ABOUT CINDY'S HAIR?

YES...ALTHOUGH THESE DAYS IT ALWAYS SEEMS TO BE SOMETHING CRUEL THAT THE LAUGHTER IS DROWNING OUT!

COME ON, LISA,...DON'T BE SO HARD ON FUNKY!

HE'S UNDER A LOT OF PRESSURE JUST WORKING HARD TO STAY ONE STEP AHEAD OF THE COMPETITION!

IT SEEMS LIKE HE'S WORKING HARD TO STAY ONE STEP AHEAD OF TOTALLY LOSING IT!

BECKY AND RACHEL WERE ALMOST MUGGED TRYING TO DELIVER A PIZZA!?

UH, HUH ... WE PICKED IT UP ON THE POLICE SCANNER... BUT APPARENTLY THEY HAD BEEN TAKING TAE-BO KICKBOXING CLASSES AT COMMUNITY COLLEGE...

AND THEY REALLY GIRL-HANDLED THEIR ATTACKERS!

WE HAVE SPECIAL SOFTWARE ON OUR COMPUTERS THAT WE USE TO FLAG HIGH-CRIME-RATE AREAS!

BECKY AND RACHEL SHOULD NEVER HAVE GONE OUT ON A DELIVERY WITHOUT CHECKING THE COMPUTER FIRST... WHEN I THINK ABOUT WHAT COULD'VE HAPPENED...

THE LAST THING I NEED IS BAD PUBLICITY!

FOR A SECOND THERE I THOUGHT YOU MIGHT ACTUALLY HAVE BEEN CONCERNED ABOUT WHAT COULD'VE HAPPENED TO BECKY AND RACHEL ...

YOU'RE SO SELF-ABSORBED AND WRAPPED UP IN THIS BUSINESS...THAT YOU CAN'T THINK ABOUT ANYTHING OR ANYONE ELSE!

OH, AND BY THE WAY... HAPPY ANNIVERSARY!

OH, AND BY THE WAY... HAPPY ANNIVERSARY!

AND YOU SAY THAT MONTONI'S HAS A DATABASE THAT TAKES CERTAIN NEIGHBORHOODS OUT OF PLAY BECAUSE THEY'RE DANGEROUS?

THAT'S RIGHT!

THEN THIS ISN'T A STORY ABOUT AN ATTEMPTED MUGGING OF A PIZZA DELIVERY PERSON...

IT'S NOT?

NO... IT'S ABOUT REDLINING!

THE LAST THING I NEED IS BAD PUBLICITY!

I DON'T THINK A PIECE ON REDLINING IS SUCH A GOOD IDEA!

LISTEN, OUR VIEWERS HAVE A RIGHT TO KNOW WHAT'S HAPPENING IN THEIR NEIGHBORHOODS!

BESIDES... IF THIS GETS PICKED UP NATIONALLY... IT COULD BE YOUR BIG BREAK!

OR MY BIG BREAK-UP!

I got these from a local nursery... Sorry about our anniversary! Meet me at...

BATIUK
8-7

COULD YOU TELL ME WHAT ROOM MR. WINKERBEAN IS IN?

CERTAINLY!

AND THERE'S THIS PACKAGE FOR YOU!

8-8

VICTO
SECR

THANKS FOR COMING!

WHAT WOMAN COULD RESIST AN INVITATION THAT RHYMES NURSERY WITH ANNIVERSARY?

HOW ABOUT A LITTLE SOMETHING TO HELP US RELAX?

BATIUK

I'VE GOT A BETTER WAY TO HELP YOU RELAX!

8-9

YOU KNOW, CIN... WE'RE BOTH TRYING TO GET ESTABLISHED IN OUR CAREERS RIGHT NOW AND SOMETIMES IT MAKES MARRIED LIFE KIND OF TENSE...

BUT DON'T WORRY, KID... WE'LL GET THROUGH IT!

I HOPE SO... BUT IT DOESN'T SEEM THAT MARRIAGE IS SOMETHING YOU SHOULD HAVE TO GET THROUGH!

SO WHAT STORY ARE YOU WORKING ON NOW, CIN?

UH... IT'S UH... A PIECE ABOUT THE PIZZA BUSINESS IN TOWN!

WELL, DON'T FORGET ABOUT YOUR FAVORITE PIZZERIA!

WELL, I SUPPOSE WE'D BETTER GET BACK TO WORK!

I SUPPOSE...

I'VE FINISHED THE LEGWORK ON THAT REDLINING STORY INVOLVING THE PIZZA DELIVERY PLACES... BUT I'D RATHER LET SOMEONE ELSE REPORT IT!

BECAUSE YOUR HUSBAND OWNS A PIZZA PLACE AND YOU FEEL IT WOULD BE A CONFLICT OF INTEREST?

NO... BECAUSE I'M NOT INTERESTED IN ANY MORE CONFLICTS WITH MY HUSBAND!

10-2

ALL RIGHT, CINDY, I'LL TAKE YOU OFF THE REDLINING PIECE... BUT IT COULD'VE BEEN A BIG STORY FOR YOU!

NEWS DIRECTOR

10-3

OH, I'M SURE ANOTHER BIG STORY WILL COME ALONG...

CHANNEL SEVEN

SO THIS IS THE ARTICLE THAT THE GIRL WHO GOT SUSPENDED WROTE?

Scapegoatzette
The Dark Side of High School

YEAH... I THOUGHT IT WAS A VERY HONEST AND BRAVE PIECE!

10-4

I SUPPOSE... BUT YOU KNOW, THERE'S KIND OF A THIN LINE BETWEEN PUSHING THE ENVELOPE AND PUSHING YOUR LUCK!

Scapegoat
The Dark T of H

YOUR JOURNALISM STUDENT REALLY SHOWED WHAT IT'S LIKE FOR KIDS WHO AREN'T CONSIDERED POPULAR... AND I WANT TO DO A PIECE ON HER SUSPENSION!

GOOD, BUT I HAVE TO ASK... ARE YOU DOING THIS OUT OF FRIENDSHIP OR CONVICTION?

BOTH...

... BUT MOSTLY OUT OF GUILT!

FOR YOUR INFORMATION, BEING THE MOST POPULAR GIRL AT WESTVIEW HIGH WASN'T ALWAYS ALL IT WAS CRACKED UP TO BE!

OH, YEAH... IN WHAT WAY?

I'M THINKING, YOU RAT!

TAKE YOUR TIME!

THANKS FOR AGREEING TO DO THE STORY, CINDY... I KNOW HOW BUSY...

HEY, IT COMES WITH THE TERRITORY!

I'M SO INVOLVED IN OTHER PEOPLE'S LIVES...

I'M BARELY INVOLVED IN MY OWN...

ATTORNEYS FOR THE YOUNG STUDENT ARE EXPECTED TO FIGHT THE SUSPENSION!

WAY TO GO, CIN!

THANKS, CINDY!

UP NEXT...

ARE LOCAL PIZZA DELIVERY OPERATIONS PRACTICING REDLINING?

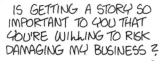

IS GETTING A STORY SO IMPORTANT TO YOU THAT YOU'RE WILLING TO RISK DAMAGING MY BUSINESS?

FOR YOUR INFORMATION, I MADE SURE THE STORY COVERED ALL THE PIZZA PLACES IN TOWN... BEFORE I ASKED TO BE REMOVED FROM IT!!

MAYBE THOSE TWO SHOULD CONSIDER SWITCHING TO DECAF!

LOOK, WE NEED TO TALK!

FINE... AS SOON AS I POUR MYSELF A DRINK!

FINE!

THESE DAYS IT SEEMS LIKE YOU'D RATHER HAVE A DRINK THAN A DISCUSSION!

13

YOU KNOW WHAT THIS IS REALLY ABOUT!? IT'S ABOUT MY JOB!!

YOU JUST CAN'T HANDLE THE FACT THAT I'M DOING SO WELL AND THAT A WOMAN IS GETTING THE BEST OF YOU!!

ASSUMING THERE'S STILL A BEST OF YOU LEFT TO GET!

YOU'RE GOING TO HAVE TO DECIDE IF YOU'RE MARRIED TO ME OR TO THAT JOB OF YOURS!!

YOU'RE A FINE ONE TO TALK ABOUT BEING CHAINED TO A JOB!!

YOU SPEND MORE TIME HERE THAN...

BEEP! BEEP!

ALL RIGHT... I'LL BE THERE AS SOON AS I CAN!

I'VE GOT TO RUN... WE'LL FINISH THIS LATER!

IN THE MEANTIME... I'LL FINISH THIS NOW!

LET'S RAISE A GLASS OF BEAUJOLAIS NOUVEAU TO THE ANNIVERSARY COUPLE ... THEN TO HALLOWEEN ... AND THEN TO DAYLIGHT SAVINGS TIME ...

WHOA ... SLOW DOWN, PAL !

AT THE RATE YOU'RE GOING ... YOU'RE LIABLE TO DEPLETE THIS YEAR'S GRAPE HARVEST !

SERIOUSLY !? FOR A SPOT ON 'ABC WORLD NEWS OVERNIGHT' ? OKAY, FINE ... I'LL WAIT TO HEAR FROM YOU !

WOW! ABC IS INTERESTED IN ME !!

UH, OH ... ABC IS INTERESTED IN ME !

WHAT ARE YOU DOING HERE IN THE MIDDLE OF THE DAY ?

I WAS ABLE TO PULL AWAY FROM THE STATION FOR A BIT AND THOUGHT MAYBE WE COULD GRAB A LATE LUNCH !

KNOW ANY GOOD PLACES TO EAT ?

SO ABC IN NEW YORK IS INTERESTED IN YOU?

UH, HUH ... I CAN'T TELL YOU HOW EXCITED I AM JUST TO KNOW THEY'RE INTERESTED IN ME!

11-29

YOU USED TO BE EXCITED BY THE FACT THAT **I** WAS INTERESTED IN YOU!

LOOK, FUNKY ... I KNOW YOU'RE WORRIED ABOUT HOW A JOB OFFER FROM NEW YORK MIGHT AFFECT OUR LIVES ...

BUT, BELIEVE ME ... IT'S NOT GOING TO COME BETWEEN ...

BEEEP! BEEEP!

11-30

JUST A SEC ...

THEY **DID!?** AND THEY WANT ME TO COME TO NEW YORK!? I DON'T **BELIEVE** IT!!

12-1

OKAY ... CALL ME WHEN YOU HAVE THE DETAILS WORKED OUT!

CONGRATULATIONS ...

TRUST ME, FUNKY ... THIS JOB OFFER FROM NEW YORK ISN'T GOING TO CHANGE ANYTHING!
THINGS BETWEEN US ARE GOING TO STAY JUST THE WAY THEY ARE!
THAT'S WHAT SCARES ME!
12-2
BATIUK

WHY DID I HAVE TO ARGUE WITH FUNKY BEFORE I LEFT ?
YOU KNOW, FUNKY... I MAY NOT EVEN GET THIS JOB IN NEW YORK !
ISN'T IT A LITTLE EARLY IN THE DAY FOR THAT ?
IT'S ONE IN THE MORNING IN SRI LANKA... BE CREATIVE, CINDY !
ARE YOU SURE YOU DON'T WANT A DRINK ?
BATIUK
12-3
I SAID WOULD YOU LIKE SOMETHING TO DRINK ?
UH, NO THANKS !

I'LL TELL YOU, FUNKY... E-COMMERCE IS KILLING MY BACK!

HAPPY HOUR ALREADY?

JUST A LITTLE SOMETHING FOR THE SUNDAY BLUES!

BUT IT'S MONDAY MORNING!

DON'T GET TECHNICAL!

MR. WINKERBEAN... I HAVE SOME SUGGESTIONS FOR CHANGES IN THE MENU!

LISTEN, CARLO, OLD BUDDY... I HAPPEN TO BE THE CO-OWNER OF THIS RESTAURANT AND AS FAR AS I'M CONCERNED... THE MENU IS JUST PEACHY THE WAY IT IS!

WELL, I NEVER!!

WELL MAYBE YOU SHOULD!

WHAT DID YOU SAY TO CARLO? I FOUND THIS NOTE IN THE KITCHEN SAYING THAT HE'S RESIGNED!

WE JUST HAD A LITTLE ARGUMENT, THAT'S ALL!

WHAT ARE WE GOING TO DO, TONY? THE HOLIDAYS ARE OUR BUSIEST TIME... WE'LL NEVER FIND A GOOD COOK ON SUCH SHORT NOTICE!!

I DID ALL THE COOKING HERE ONCE... I CAN DO IT AGAIN!

I REST MY CASE!

TONY, I'M REALLY SORRY ABOUT ALL OF THIS... HERE, LET ME HELP!

CRAASH!!

12-7

I THINK YOU'VE DONE QUITE ENOUGH ALREADY!

I THINK THE BEST PLACE FOR YOU RIGHT NOW IS AT HOME...!

12-8

BEFORE I START RETHINKING THIS WHOLE PARTNERSHIP THING!

YOU'RE IN NO CONDITION TO DRIVE HOME... SO I CALLED YOU A CAB!

OKAY... I'M A CAB!

WHERE TO, BUDDY?

TAKE ME AROUND TO THE BACK OF MONTONI'S!

TAXI

YELLER CAB CO.

THANK YOU, MY GOOD MAN...

TAXI

I'LL TAKE IT FROM HERE!

SUIT YOURSELF, PAL... IT'S YOUR FUNERAL!

YELLER CAB CO.

12-9

IT'S A GOOD THING I KEEP THIS BACK HERE FOR EMERGENCIES!

THE NERVE OF TONY THINKING THAT I'M TOO DRUNKY DRUNK TO DRIVE HOME!

IN FACT, I'D BE THERE ALREADY IF THE TRAFFIC WASN'T SO BAD!

OHHH...

:CLICK:
WITH THE RAIN TURNING TO SNOW...

MAN... MY HEAD FEELS LIKE IT'S GOING TO BUST...

BY LATER IN THE DAY!

12-11

I WONDER IF I SAID OR DID ANYTHING OUT OF LINE LAST NIGHT?

IN OTHER NEWS... POLICE ARE LOOKING FOR A HIT-SKIP DRIVER WHO...

THE LITTLE GIRL WHO WAS STRUCK...

12-12

WAS IN THE CROSSWALK! THE WHEREABOUTS OF THE HIT-SKIP DRIVER ARE...

DON'T PANIC!

THERE'S PROBABLY A PERFECTLY GOOD EXPLANATION FOR WHY THE CAR'S NOT IN THE GARAGE!

12-13

IF I COULD ONLY REMEMBER WHAT IT WAS!

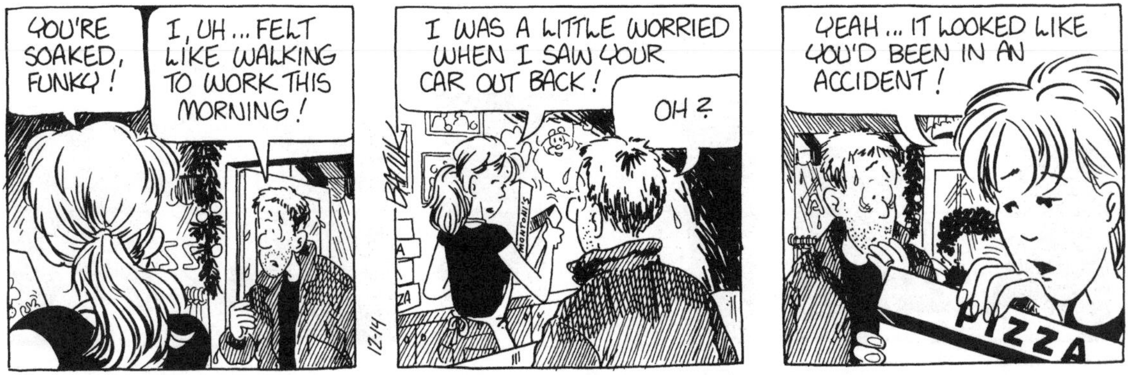
YOU'RE SOAKED, FUNKY!
I, UH... FELT LIKE WALKING TO WORK THIS MORNING!
I WAS A LITTLE WORRIED WHEN I SAW YOUR CAR OUT BACK!
OH?
YEAH... IT LOOKED LIKE YOU'D BEEN IN AN ACCIDENT!
PIZZA
12-14

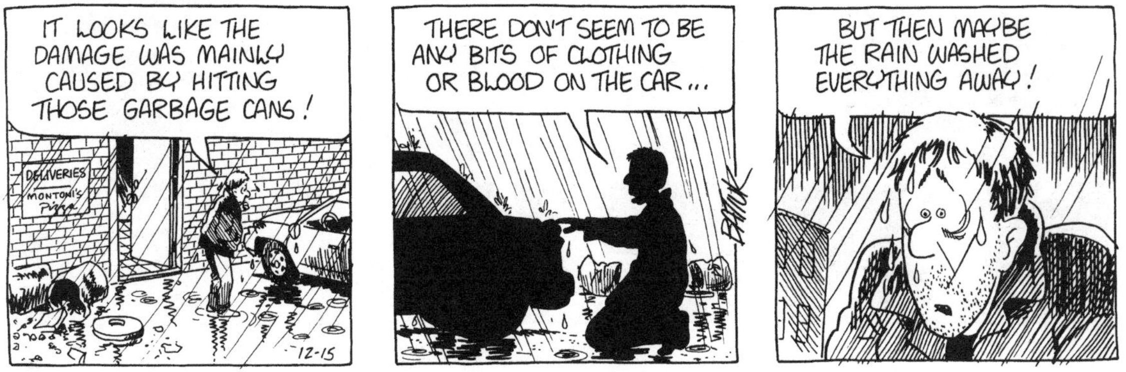
IT LOOKS LIKE THE DAMAGE WAS MAINLY CAUSED BY HITTING THOSE GARBAGE CANS!
DELIVERIES
MONTONI'S Pizza
12-15
THERE DON'T SEEM TO BE ANY BITS OF CLOTHING OR BLOOD ON THE CAR...
BUT THEN MAYBE THE RAIN WASHED EVERYTHING AWAY!

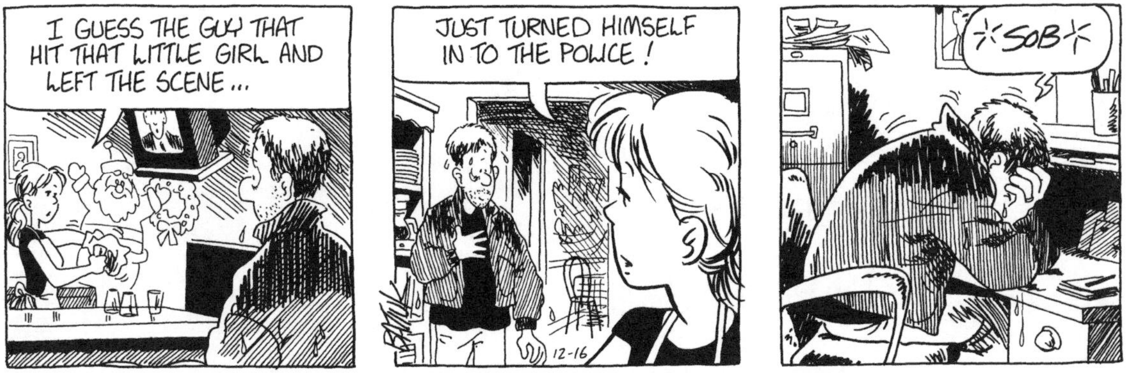
I GUESS THE GUY THAT HIT THAT LITTLE GIRL AND LEFT THE SCENE...
JUST TURNED HIMSELF IN TO THE POLICE!
12-16
SOB

I HAVEN'T BEEN MYSELF LATELY... BEEN DRINKING A LITTLE MORE THAN I SHOULD...

AND I KNOW I'VE LET YOU DOWN!

THE THING IS... I WANT YOU TO KNOW I DON'T HAVE A DRINKING PROBLEM...

IT'S JUST THAT I'VE BEEN UNDER A LOT OF STRESS LATELY... RUNNING THE RESTAURANT, DEALING WITH MY MARRIAGE, THE PRESSURE OF THE HOLIDAYS...

BUT I WANT TO ASSURE YOU THAT WHAT HAPPENED THE OTHER DAY WAS JUST AN ISOLATED INCIDENT... TOMORROW'S GOING TO BE DIFFERENT... I PROMISE...

REALLY... I PROMISE!

BATIUK

12-17

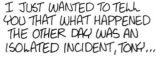 I JUST WANTED TO TELL YOU THAT WHAT HAPPENED THE OTHER DAY WAS AN ISOLATED INCIDENT, TONY...

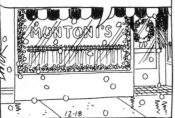

12-18

AND THAT YOU DON'T HAVE TO WORRY ABOUT ME... I'M FINE!

I GUESS I JUST GOT INTO THE HOLIDAY SPIRITS A LITTLE TOO MUCH... GET IT? | UH, HUH... I JUST HOPE THAT YOU GET IT!

IT LOOKS LIKE OUR REGULAR HAS DOZED OFF AGAIN RIGHT ON SCHEDULE!

EVERY NIGHT HE COMES IN HERE ABOUT AN HOUR BEFORE CLOSING... DRINKS HIMSELF INTO A STUPOR... AND THEN FALLS ASLEEP!

I MAY DRINK A LITTLE, BUT I GUESS I'M OKAY... BECAUSE I'M NOT THERE YET!

12-19

TIME TO HEAD ON HOME, PAL! CAN I CALL YOU A CAB? I DON'T THINK YOU SHOULD BE DRIVING!

12-20

DON'T WORRY... I'M NOT ONE OF THOSE GUYS WHO GETS BEHIND THE OL' WHEELIE IF HE'S HAD A LITTLE TOO MUCH TO DRINK!

I'M OKAY... I'M NOT THERE YET!

IT'S BEEN TWO WHOLE DAYS SINCE I'VE HAD A DRINK... THIS CALLS FOR A CELEBRATION...

12-21

WITH COFFEE OF COURSE... ALTHOUGH IT'S KIND OF LATE FOR COFFEE...

TONI'S

SO MAYBE JUST A SHOT OF KAHLUA TO TAKE THE EDGE OFF...

WHAT ARE YOU DOING HERE SO EARLY? OH, OH...

I GUESS I SHOULD BE ASKING WHAT YOU'RE DOING HERE SO LATE?

GREAT? YOU BET I FEEL GREAT!

I'VE FINALLY CONQUERED MY @#&%*# WILLPOWER!

12-22

YOU'RE DRUNK AGAIN!

BINGO! WHERE'S MY BOX OF GOLD STARS?

I DON'T THINK IT WOULD BE SUCH A GOOD IDEA FOR TONY TO SEE YOU LIKE THIS!

NO, SIREEE... FUNKY IS DRUNKY...

AND SINCE CINDY'S OUT OF TOWN... I'D BETTER GET YOU HOME!

HOME ON THE RANGE...

O 12-23

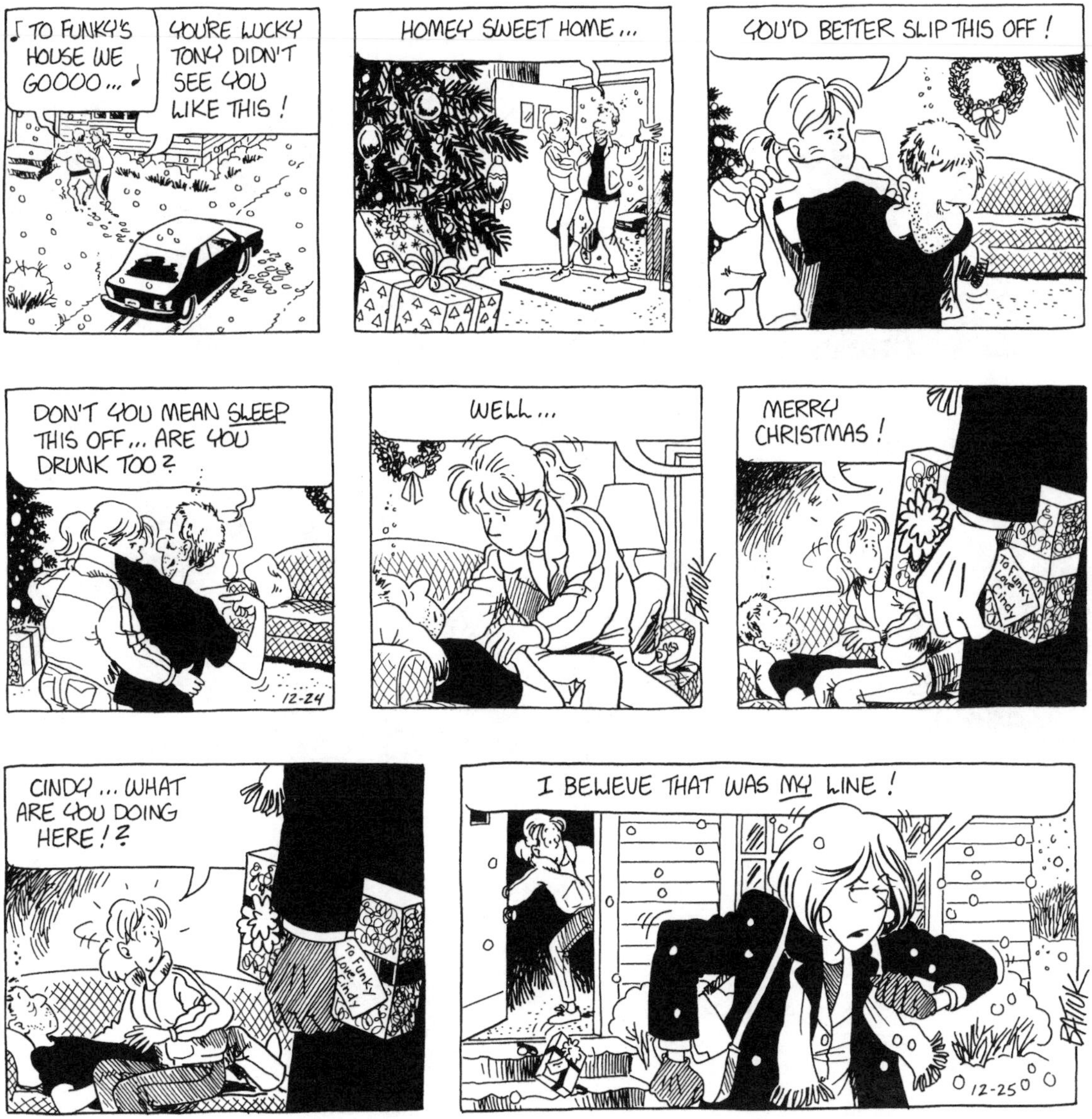
♪ TO FUNKY'S HOUSE WE GOOOO... ♪
YOU'RE LUCKY TONY DIDN'T SEE YOU LIKE THIS!
HOMEY SWEET HOME...
YOU'D BETTER SLIP THIS OFF!
DON'T YOU MEAN SLEEP THIS OFF... ARE YOU DRUNK TOO?
12-24
WELL...
BATIUK
MERRY CHRISTMAS!
To Funky Love Cindy
CINDY... WHAT ARE YOU DOING HERE!?
To Funky Love Cindy
I BELIEVE THAT WAS MY LINE!
BATIUK
12-25

GATE 12
BEEP! BEEP!
SNIFF
HELLO...
HI... IT'S ME...
12-26
BATIUK

PLEASE, CINDY... DON'T FLY BACK TO NEW YORK... AT LEAST GIVE ME A CHANCE TO EXPLAIN EVERYTHING!
ALL RIGHT... MY FLIGHT LEAVES IN FORTY-FIVE MINUTES... IF YOU'RE HERE BEFORE THEN WE'LL TALK... IF NOT, I'M LEAVING!
GATE 12
14
I'M AT GATE NUMBER TWELVE!
BATIUK
12-27

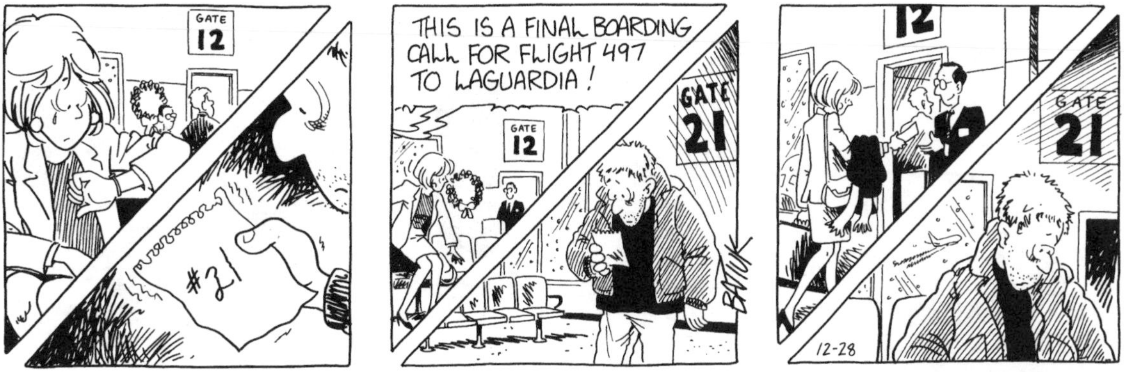
GATE 12
#21
THIS IS A FINAL BOARDING CALL FOR FLIGHT 497 TO LAGUARDIA!
GATE 12
GATE 21
BATIUK
12
GATE 21
12-28

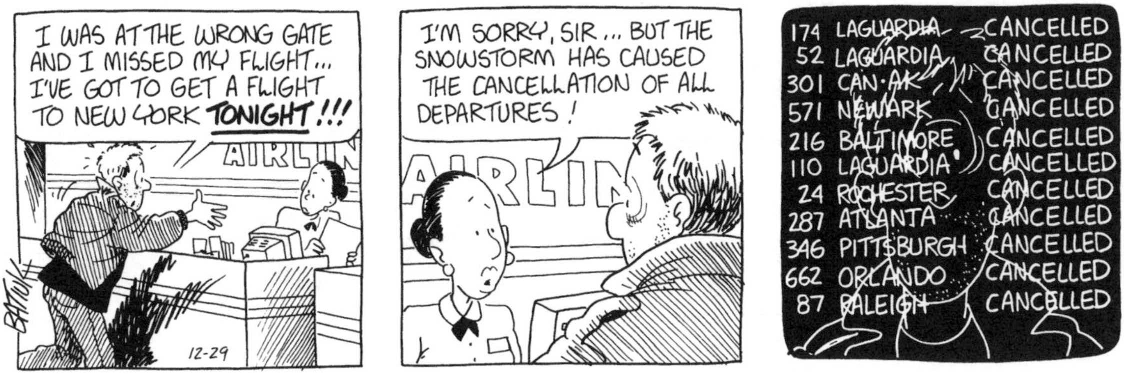
I WAS AT THE WRONG GATE AND I MISSED MY FLIGHT... I'VE GOT TO GET A FLIGHT TO NEW YORK **TONIGHT**!!!
BATIUK
12-29
I'M SORRY, SIR... BUT THE SNOWSTORM HAS CAUSED THE CANCELLATION OF ALL DEPARTURES!
174 LAGUARDIA CANCELLED
52 LAGUARDIA CANCELLED
301 CAN-AK CANCELLED
571 NEWARK CANCELLED
216 BALTIMORE CANCELLED
110 LAGUARDIA CANCELLED
24 ROCHESTER CANCELLED
287 ATLANTA CANCELLED
346 PITTSBURGH CANCELLED
662 ORLANDO CANCELLED
87 RALEIGH CANCELLED

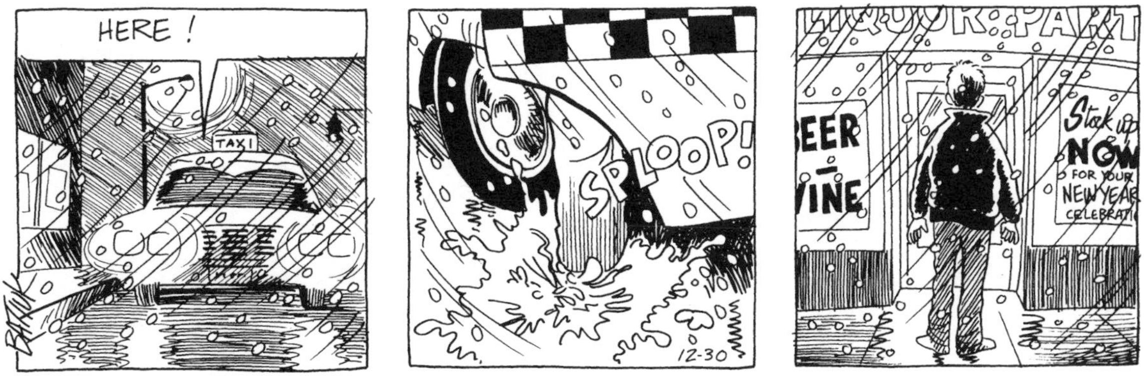
HERE!
TAXI
BATIUK
SPLOOP!
12-30
FOR YOUR

TONI'S
HAPPY NEW YEAR
BATIUK
12-31

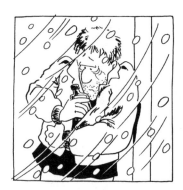

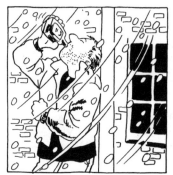

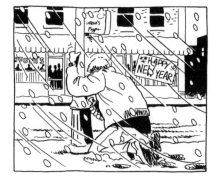

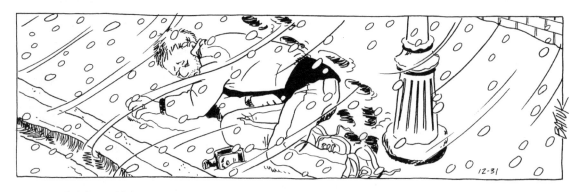

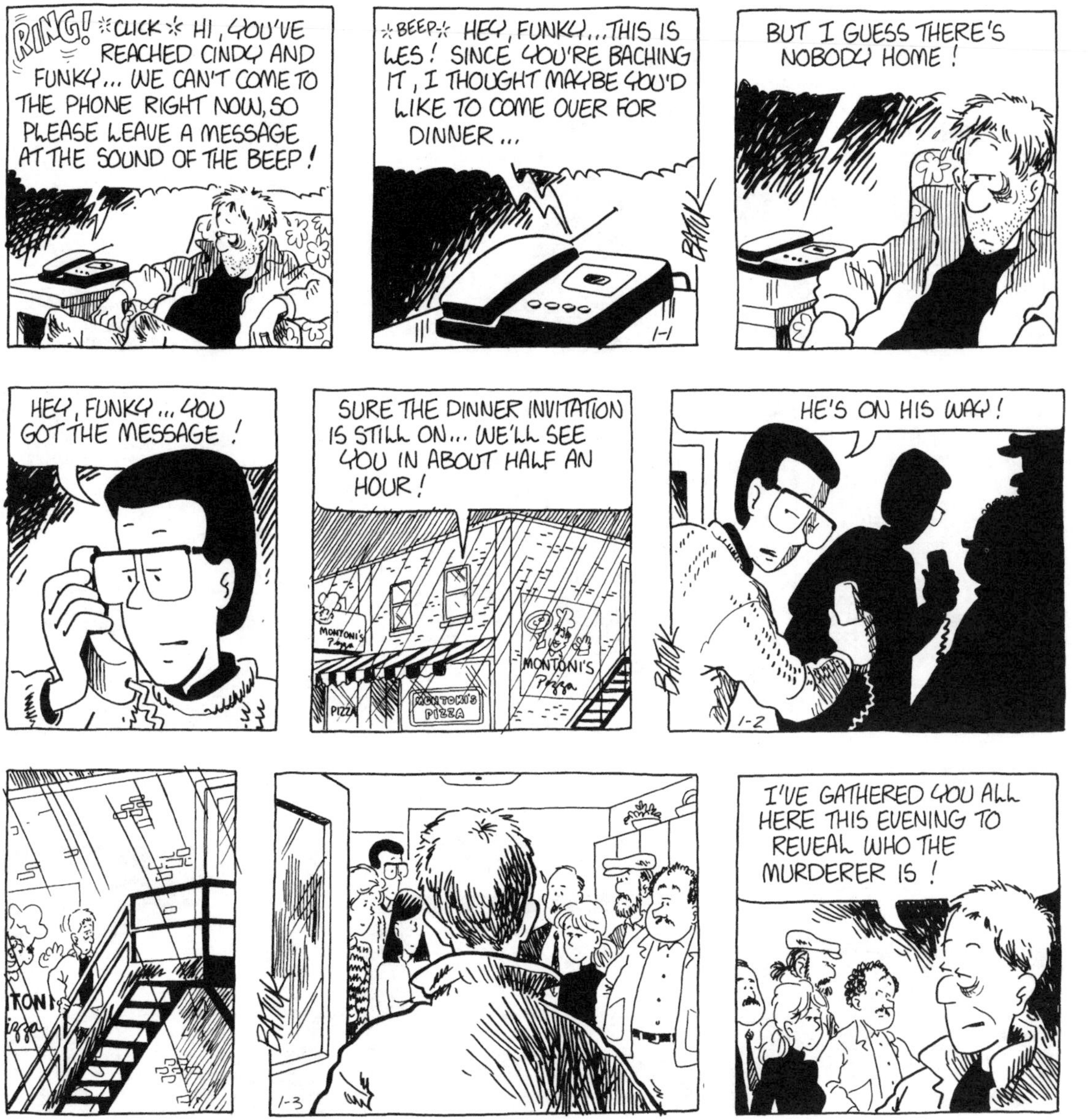
RING! *CLICK* HI, YOU'VE REACHED CINDY AND FUNKY... WE CAN'T COME TO THE PHONE RIGHT NOW, SO PLEASE LEAVE A MESSAGE AT THE SOUND OF THE BEEP!
BEEP HEY, FUNKY... THIS IS LES! SINCE YOU'RE BACHING IT, I THOUGHT MAYBE YOU'D LIKE TO COME OVER FOR DINNER...
BATIUK
1-1
BUT I GUESS THERE'S NOBODY HOME!
HEY, FUNKY... YOU GOT THE MESSAGE!
SURE THE DINNER INVITATION IS STILL ON... WE'LL SEE YOU IN ABOUT HALF AN HOUR!
MONTONI'S Pizza
MONTONI'S Pizza
PIZZA
MONTONI'S PIZZA
HE'S ON HIS WAY!
BATIUK
1-2
BATIUK
1-3
I'VE GATHERED YOU ALL HERE THIS EVENING TO REVEAL WHO THE MURDERER IS!

FUNKY, THIS IS DR. BENNET... HE'S A CHEMICAL DEPENDENCY COUNSELOR WHO'S DEALT WITH PROBLEMS LIKE YOURS, AND HE HELPED ME TO SET UP THIS INTERVENTION!

AND IT LOOKS LIKE WE HAVE PERFECT ATTENDANCE TOO! IS CINDY HIDING SOMEWHERE...?

OR COULDN'T MY SIGNIFICANT MOTHER MAKE IT?

I REALLY HATE TO DISAPPOINT YOU FOLKS... BUT I DON'T HAVE A DRINKING PROBLEM!

AU CONTRAIRE, AMIGO... YOU'VE BEEN PRETTY MESSED UP LATELY AND ACTING LIKE A REAL JERK!

NOT TO MENTION MAKING A MESS OF THINGS AT WORK!

REMEMBER... BE UNDERSTANDING AND NON-JUDGMENTAL!

ALTHOUGH WE DON'T NECESSARILY MEAN THAT IN A BAD WAY!

YOUR FRIENDS AND COLLEAGUES ARE SIMPLY URGING YOU TO GET HELP... BUT THAT'S SOMETHING YOU NEED TO BE READY TO DO!

KEEP IN MIND, THOUGH, THAT THE WALL YOU PUT UP TO PROTECT YOURSELF FROM THE PAIN...

IS THE SAME ONE THAT KEEPS THE PAIN IN!

YOUR FRIENDS HAVE INITIATED THIS INTERVENTION TO URGE YOU TO GET HELP...

WHETHER YOU CHOOSE TO DO SO OR NOT IS UP TO YOU!

IF YOU WANT TO BLAME SOMEONE, BLAME ME...THIS INTERVENTION WAS MY IDEA!

1-7

BUT BEFORE YOU GO...THIS IS A RESERVATION FOR YOU AT THE PINEBROOK REHABILITATION CLINIC!

LES, YOU'RE MY SECOND BEST FRIEND IN THE WHOLE WORLD...WANT TO KNOW WHO THE FIRST IS?

ANYONE ELSE!

THANKS FOR THE RESERVATION TO THE REHAB CLINIC!

SLAM!

I'LL BE SURE TO PASS IT ALONG TO SOMEONE WHO NEEDS IT!

1-8

THAT WENT WELL... DON'T YOU THINK?

HELLO, UNCLE...

WALLY! SO LES ENLISTED YOU FOR HIS LITTLE INTERVENTION PARTY TOO, HUH?

1-9

UH, HUH... BUT I COULDN'T DO IT!

WELL, AT LEAST I HAVE ONE FRIEND LEFT IN THE WORLD!

ACTUALLY... HE TOLD ME THAT BECKY WOULD BE THERE AND I JUST COULDN'T FACE HER AGAIN!

I STILL HAVE NIGHTMARES ABOUT THE NIGHT OF THE ACCIDENT!

1-10

THE CAR ROLLED OVER THREE TIMES AND THEY HAD TO USE THE JAWS OF LIFE TO PULL US FROM THE WRECKAGE... I'LL NEVER FORGIVE MYSELF FOR WHAT HAPPENED TO BECKY'S ARM... HER CAREER PLANS...

AND I'LL NEVER TOUCH ANOTHER DROP OF ALCOHOL ...OR ANOTHER WOMAN!

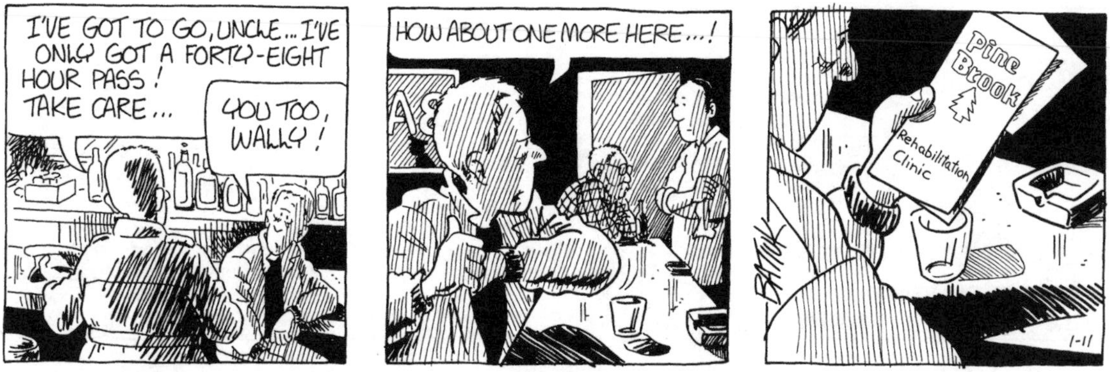
I'VE GOT TO GO, UNCLE... I'VE ONLY GOT A FORTY-EIGHT HOUR PASS! TAKE CARE...
YOU TOO, WALLY!
HOW ABOUT ONE MORE HERE...!
Pine Brook
Rehabilitation Clinic
BATIUK
1-11

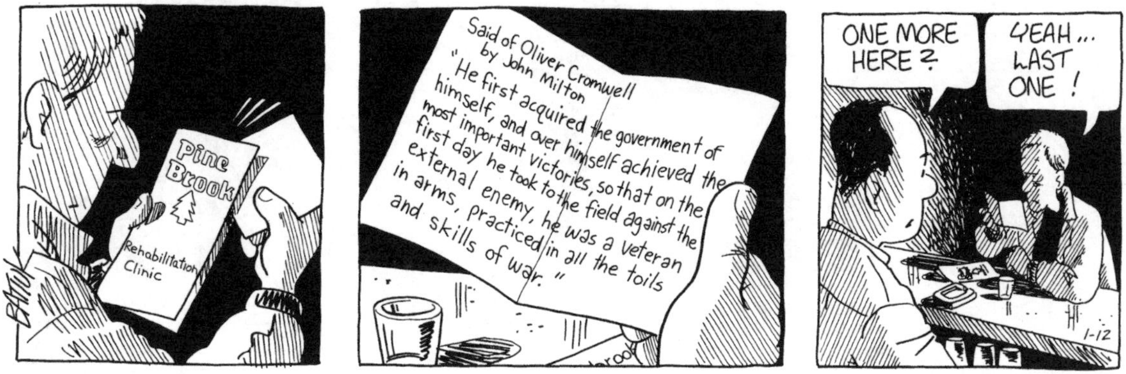
Pine Brook
Rehabilitation Clinic
BATIUK
Said of Oliver Cromwell by John Milton
"He first acquired the government of himself, and over himself achieved the most important victories, so that on the first day he took to the field against the external enemy, he was a veteran in arms, practiced in all the toils and skills of war."
ONE MORE HERE?
YEAH... LAST ONE!
1-12

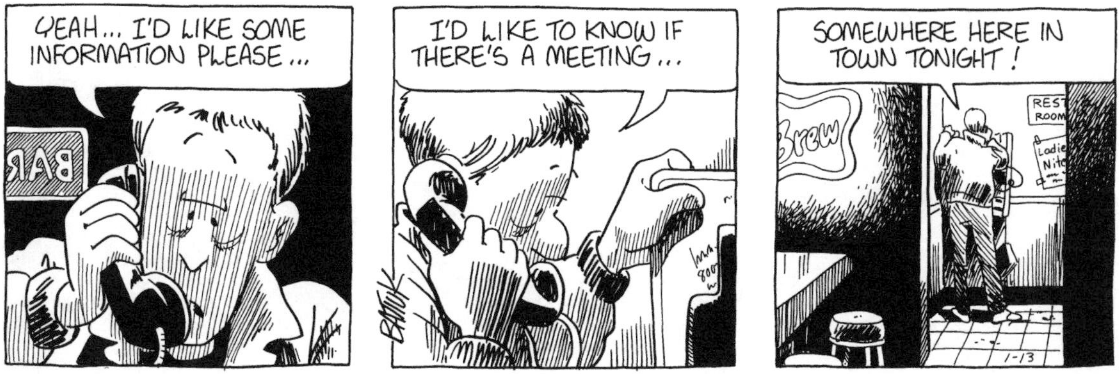
YEAH... I'D LIKE SOME INFORMATION PLEASE...
I'D LIKE TO KNOW IF THERE'S A MEETING...
BATIUK
SOMEWHERE HERE IN TOWN TONIGHT!
Brew
REST ROOM
1-13

I'D LIKE TO KNOW IF THERE'S A MEETING SOMEWHERE HERE IN TOWN TONIGHT!

ACCORDING TO PEOPLE AT AA... THE PLACE WHERE THE MEETING IS BEING HELD SHOULD BE SOMEWHERE ON THIS BLOCK!

AA DOWNTOWN
TWELVE & TWELVE
MEETING
8:00

YOU CAN JUST HAVE A SEAT ANYWHERE!

GOT ANYTHING IN THE NON-SMOKING SECTION?

1-15

WADE!

SURPRISED TO SEE ME HERE?

1-16

NO... I'M SURPRISED TO SEE ME HERE!

I'M NOT SURE I BELONG AT AN AA MEETING, WADE... I SUPPOSE I HAVE A PROBLEM, BUT IT'S NOT THAT BAD YET!

RIGHT... THE 'YETS'... ALL THE HORRIBLE THINGS YOU COULD'VE DONE, BUT HAVEN'T DONE YET!

Happy Holidays

AA DOWNTOWN TWELVE & TWELVE

IN AA, WE SAY THAT 'YET' STANDS FOR 'YOU'RE ELIGIBLE TOO'!

1-17

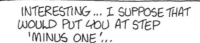

I KNOW YOU'VE HAD A PROBLEM WITH ALCOHOL FOR A LONG TIME, WADE... BUT I DON'T THINK THAT MINE'S AS BAD AS YOURS!

INTERESTING... I SUPPOSE THAT WOULD PUT YOU AT STEP 'MINUS ONE'...

ADMITTING THAT OTHERS ARE ALCOHOLICS!

I SUPPOSE I STARTED BINGING ON ALCOHOL WHEN I WAS IN COLLEGE...

AA DOWNTOWN TWELVE & TWELVE

'BUT I JUST WANTED TO BE LIKE EVERYONE ELSE!'

AND YOU SUCCEEDED... YOU'RE LIKE ALL OF US!

ONE DAY AT A TIME

LET'S GO AROUND THE TABLE AND INTRODUCE OURSELVES!

I'M GWEN... I'M AN ALCOHOLIC!

HI, GWEN!

I'M BILL... I'M AN ALCOHOLIC!

HI, BILL!

I'M WADE... I'M AN ALCOHOLIC!

HI, WADE!

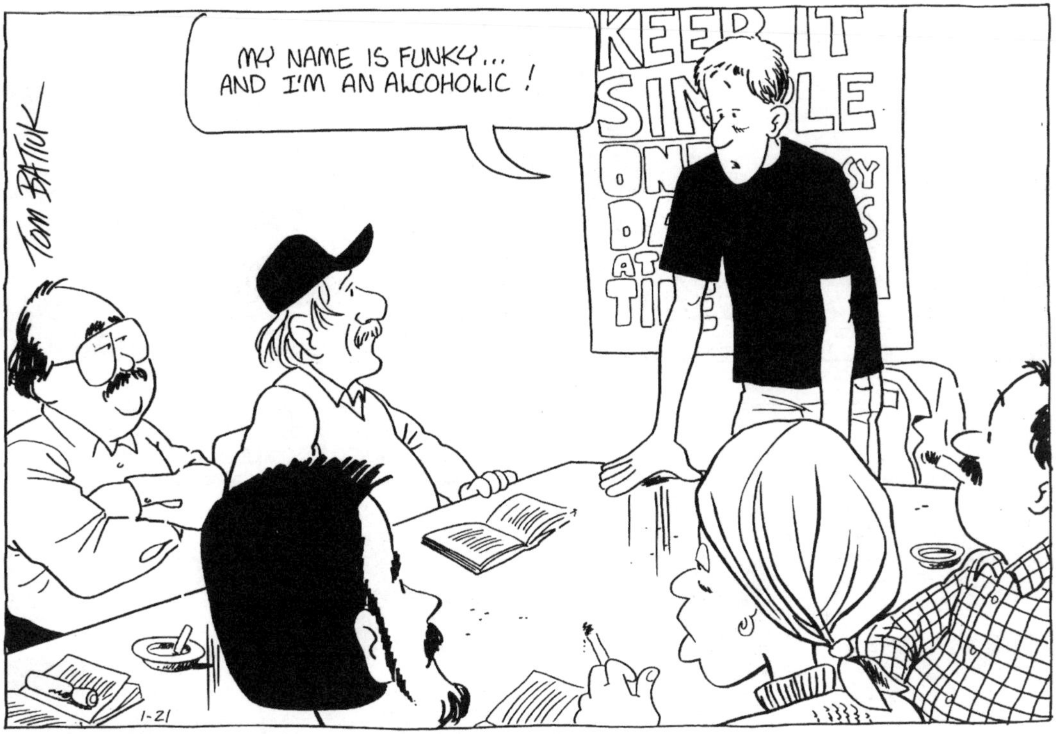
MY NAME IS FUNKY...
AND I'M AN ALCOHOLIC !
TOM BATIUK
1-21

I REPEAT... MY NAME'S FUNKY AND I'M AN ALCOHOLIC!

The TWELVE STEPS   The TWELVE TRADITIONS

I HAD TO SAY THAT TWICE BECAUSE I'M STILL GETTING USED TO THE IDEA!

1-22

ARE THERE ANY ANNIVERSARIES TO CELEBRATE TONIGHT?

AA DOWNTOWN TWELVE & TWELVE

I'M SALLY... AN ALCOHOLIC, AND I'VE BEEN SOBER THREE YEARS!

I'M TERRY...AND I'M AN ALCOHOLIC WHO'S BEEN SOBER FOR A YEAR!

Easy Does

I'M FUNKY... AN ALCOHOLIC, AND I'VE BEEN SOBER FOR ABOUT A HALF HOUR!

ONE DAY AT A TIME

1-23

ABOUT A HALF HOUR AGO I WAS SITTING ALONE IN A BAR FEELING LIKE I'D LOST EVERY FRIEND I'D EVER HAD... I WAS DESPERATELY UNHAPPY!

IT'S FUNNY... I ALWAYS THOUGHT I DRANK BECAUSE I WAS UNHAPPY... AND THEN I SUDDENLY REALIZED THAT MAYBE I WAS UNHAPPY BECAUSE I DRANK...

1-24

SO I HAD ONE LAST ONE FOR THE ROAD... THE ROAD BACK!

12 STEPS

THIS DOWNTOWN TWELVE AND TWELVE GROUP IS A PRETTY DOWN-TO-EARTH BUNCH OF ALCOHOLICS, FUNKY!

YOU'RE NOT GOING TO FIND ANY WHINEY BANG & OLUFSEN-OWNING PROFESSIONALS HERE LOOKING FOR THEIR INNER CHILDREN!

I LIKE 'EM BECAUSE THEY ENJOY THEIR SMOKES AND SWEETS... HERE, HAVE A JELLY DONUT!

THIS IS A PRETTY BACK-TO-BASICS AA BUNCH!

THEY BELIEVE ALCOHOLICS ANONYMOUS IS FOR ALCOHOLICS... AND THAT IF YOU WANT TO TALK ABOUT OTHER FORMS OF ABUSE YOU CAN GO ON JERRY SPRINGER!

JUST A BUNCH OF GOOD FOLKS TRYING THE BEST WAY THEY KNOW HOW TO STAY SOBER!

WOULD IT BE OKAY IF I HUNG ON TO THIS BOOK UNTIL THE NEXT MEETING?

THAT'S NO PROBLEM... JUST BE SURE TO RETURN!

DON'T WORRY... I'LL RETURN YOUR BOOK!

I MEANT YOU!

HOW DID WE MANAGE TO END UP WITH THE SHORT STRAW, WADE?

LIFE JUST DOESN'T SEEM VERY FAIR!

NOBODY SAID IT WAS!

THERE'S THE OLD JOKE ABOUT A GUY WHO WAS STUCK OVERNIGHT IN A SMALL TOWN AND WHO WENT INTO A BAR LOOKING FOR SOME ENTERTAINMENT!

THERE WAS A ROULETTE WHEEL IN THE BACK AND HE STARTED PLAYING AND KEPT LOSING UNTIL A WAITRESS CAME BY AND WHISPERED... 'THE WHEEL IS CROOKED'!

HE CONTINUED TO PLAY AND LOSE UNTIL FINALLY THE WAITRESS CAME BY AGAIN AND WHISPERED... 'I SAID THE WHEEL IS CROOKED'!

HE REPLIED... 'I KNOW... BUT IT'S THE ONLY GAME IN TOWN'!

...AND THEN AFTER TONY VIRTUALLY KICKED ME OUT... CINDY LEFT ME!

HECK OF A WAY TO KICK OFF THE NEW YEAR, HUH?

1-29

REALITY HAS A WAY OF SHOWING UP ON YOUR DOORSTEP WHEN YOU LEAST WANT TO FACE IT!

YOU KNOW, WADE...I'M NOT SURE I BELIEVE EVERYTHING IN THIS TWELVE STEPS BOOK!

1-30

I WASN'T SURE EITHER...AND I'LL ADMIT THAT A LOT OF THE CONCEPTS SEEM OLD AND CREAKY...

BUT YOU DON'T COMPLAIN ABOUT THE RUST ON THE FIRE ESCAPE WHEN THE BUILDING IS BURNING!

THE JOURNEY YOU'RE ABOUT TO TAKE, FUNKY... IS GOING TO DEPEND ON WHAT SORT OF RELATIONSHIP YOU HAVE WITH A HIGHER POWER!

1-31

ACTUALLY, I DON'T THINK WE HAVE A RELATIONSHIP ANYMORE!

HE DUMPED ME A WHILE AGO AND HAS BEEN SEEING SOMEBODY ELSE!

43

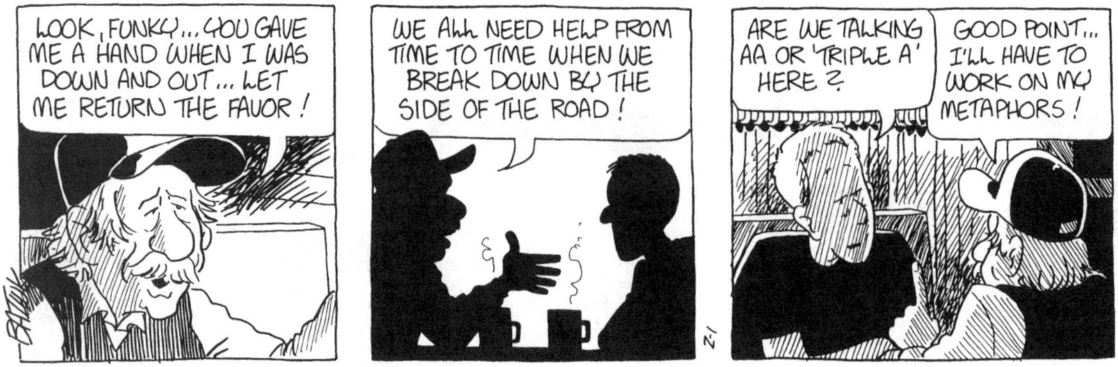
LOOK, FUNKY... YOU GAVE ME A HAND WHEN I WAS DOWN AND OUT... LET ME RETURN THE FAVOR!
WE ALL NEED HELP FROM TIME TO TIME WHEN WE BREAK DOWN BY THE SIDE OF THE ROAD!
ARE WE TALKING AA OR 'TRIPLE A' HERE?
GOOD POINT... I'LL HAVE TO WORK ON MY METAPHORS!

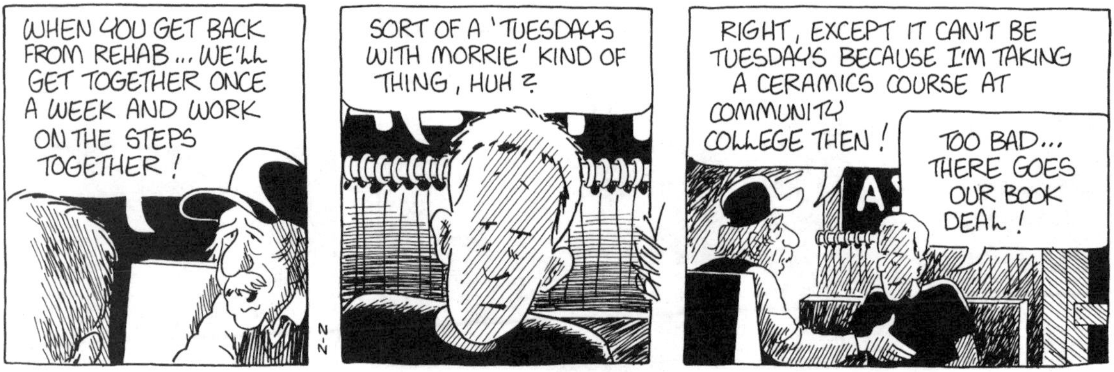
WHEN YOU GET BACK FROM REHAB... WE'LL GET TOGETHER ONCE A WEEK AND WORK ON THE STEPS TOGETHER!
SORT OF A 'TUESDAYS WITH MORRIE' KIND OF THING, HUH?
RIGHT, EXCEPT IT CAN'T BE TUESDAYS BECAUSE I'M TAKING A CERAMICS COURSE AT COMMUNITY COLLEGE THEN!
TOO BAD... THERE GOES OUR BOOK DEAL!

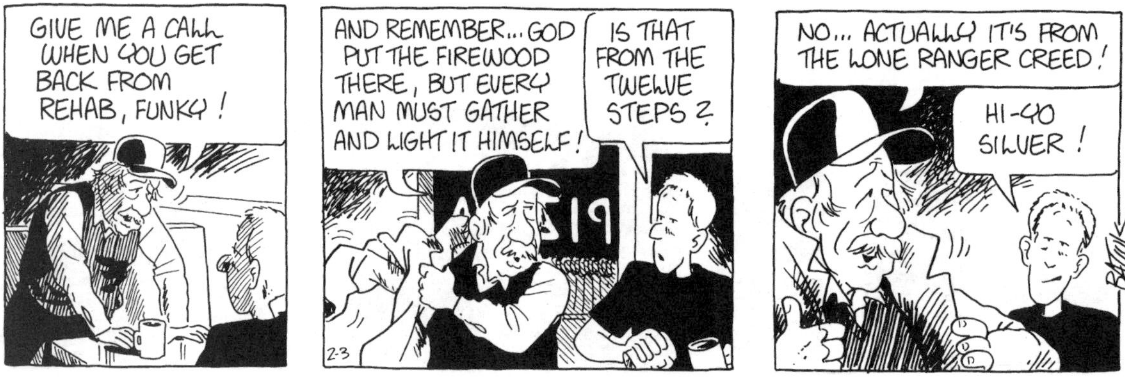
GIVE ME A CALL WHEN YOU GET BACK FROM REHAB, FUNKY!
AND REMEMBER... GOD PUT THE FIREWOOD THERE, BUT EVERY MAN MUST GATHER AND LIGHT IT HIMSELF!
IS THAT FROM THE TWELVE STEPS?
NO... ACTUALLY IT'S FROM THE LONE RANGER CREED!
HI-YO SILVER!

To Funky With all my love Cindy
THE TWELVE
READY?
AS READY AS I'LL EVER BE!
OFFICE
WHO'D HAVE THOUGHT THAT ONE DAY I'D BE CASHING IN MY FREQUENT FLIER MILES FOR AN ALL-EXPENSES-PAID VACATION AT THE DETOX MOTEL!
UNTIL RECENTLY, I'D ALWAYS THOUGHT THE 'TWELVE STEPS' WERE A MOTOWN GROUP!
MONTONI'S Pizza
I'M GLAD YOU'VE STILL GOT YOUR SENSE OF HUMOR, FUNKY... PEOPLE WERE BEGINNING TO WORRY THAT YOU'D LOST IT!
2-4

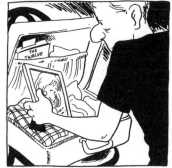

DON'T WORRY ABOUT A THING, FUNKY!

I'M NOT, TONY!

AFTER ALL, I RAN THIS PLACE ALL BY MYSELF BEFORE WE BECAME PARTNERS... AND I CAN RUN IT AGAIN THE SAME WAY!

NOW I'M WORRIED!

I'VE GOT A COUPLE BOOKS FOR YOU TO READ WHILE YOU'RE AT REHAB, FUNKY!

'THE INNER GAME OF TENNIS'?

IT'S GOT SOME GOOD POINTS TO MAKE THAT CAN BE APPLIED TO THE FIRST STEP...

ALONG WITH THE ADDED BENEFIT THAT IT MIGHT HELP YOU STRAIGHTEN OUT YOUR BACKHAND!

WHAT'S THIS OTHER BOOK... DR. SEUSS?

HE ALSO HAS SOME GOOD POINTS TO MAKE, BUT MORE IMPORTANT... HE'LL MAKE YOU LAUGH!

TRUST ME... THOSE 'NATIONAL GEOGRAPHICS' THEY HAVE THERE AT REHAB ALL START TO LOOK THE SAME AFTER A WHILE!

SO YOU'LL GET IN TOUCH WITH CINDY AND TELL HER WHAT'S GOING ON?

YOU BET!

2-8

I REALLY APPRECIATE EVERYTHING YOU'RE DOING, LES!

'TO HAVE A FRIEND A MAN MUST BE ONE!'

SHAKESPEARE?

NO, THE LONE RANGER CREED... WADE TOLD ME THAT!

I'D LIKE TO CHECK IN... MY NAME IS WINKERBEAN!

Pinebrook
REHABILITATION CENTER

2-9

I'D LIKE A NON-DRINKING ROOM, PLEASE!

inebrook
REHABILITATION CENTER

SEE YOU IN A COUPLE, PAL!

Pinebr
REHABILITA
CENTE

2-10

GREAT JOB, CINDY!

THANKS...

I'VE JUST LANDED A JOB IN NEW YORK CITY WITH A MAJOR NETWORK AND I SHOULD BE FEELING ON TOP OF THE WORLD...

3-5

INSTEAD I FEEL AS IF THE WORLD'S ON TOP OF ME!

PART OF ME WANTS THIS NETWORK JOB MORE THAN ANYTHING IN THE WORLD...

BUT ANOTHER PART OF ME DOESN'T WANT IT IF IT'S GOING TO COST ME MY MARRIAGE!

HEY... I KNOW WHO YOU ARE!

I WISH I KNEW!

3-6

I READ ABOUT YOU IN THE 'TIMES'...YOU'RE CINDY SUMMERS, THE NEW CO-ANCHOR ON 'ABC WORLD NEWS OVERNIGHT'!

THAT'S RIGHT... AND YOU ARE...

APPLE ANNIE... THE INVISIBLE WOMAN!

3-7

EXCEPT TO POLICEMEN, OF COURSE!

WATCH IT ... NO SLEEPING ON THE PARK BENCHES.

YOU'VE GOT ME THERE, OFFICER ... I'VE DEFINITELY BEEN KNOWN TO SLEEP ALL RIGHT!

3-8

IT'S OKAY ... SHE'S WITH ME!

FROM THE LOOK ON YOUR FACE ...

I'D SAY THAT THINGS BETWEEN YOU AND YOUR FELLA AREN'T AT THEIR BEST!

3-9

ACTUALLY, RIGHT NOW WE'RE DOING OUR BEST TO BE EACH OTHER'S WORST MISTAKE!

GO SEE THAT FELLA OF YOURS AND PATCH THINGS UP ...

AND DON'T WORRY ABOUT YOUR NEW JOB ... JUST BE YOURSELF!

3-10

WHICH ONE?

One month later...

READY TO GO?

READY AS I'LL EVER BE!

HOW WAS THE FOOD?

OKAY?... BUT THE WINE LIST WASN'T MUCH TO SPEAK OF!

SO HOW DID THINGS GO HERE, FUNKY?

ALL IN ALL, I'D HAVE TO SAY IT WAS A SOBERING EXPERIENCE!

A LITTLE REHAB HUMOR THERE!

SOME MIGHT EVEN CALL IT A DRY HUMOR!

3-11

CINDY! HI, LISA...

I TRIED THE APARTMENT AND NO ONE WAS THERE... I'M LOOKING FOR LES!

OH... HE'S AT THE REHABILITATION CLINIC!

ST. PADDY'S Special GREEN BEER GREEN PIZZA

3-12

LES TOO!?

OH, NO... HE'S JUST PICKING UP FUNKY TODAY!

MOM

SO RACHEL WAS JUST HELPING FUNKY GET HOME OKAY?...

AND WHEN HE TRIED TO CATCH YOU AT THE AIRPORT TO EXPLAIN... HE WENT TO THE WRONG GATE!

PIZZ

St. Patrick's Day
PARTY

AND HERE... AS MY OLD SCHOOL BUS DRIVER USED TO SAY... I THOUGHT I'D CAUGHT HIM DEAD TO WRONG!

3-13

I ENDED UP POURING OUT MY HEART ABOUT FUNKY TO THIS HOMELESS WOMAN IN CENTRAL PARK...

AND IT MADE ME REALIZE THAT I STILL LOVED HIM... AND STILL WANTED TO BE MARRIED TO HIM...

3-14

BUT MAYBE HE FEELS THAT THE GOVERNOR HAS JUST COMMUTED HIS LIFE SENTENCE!

51

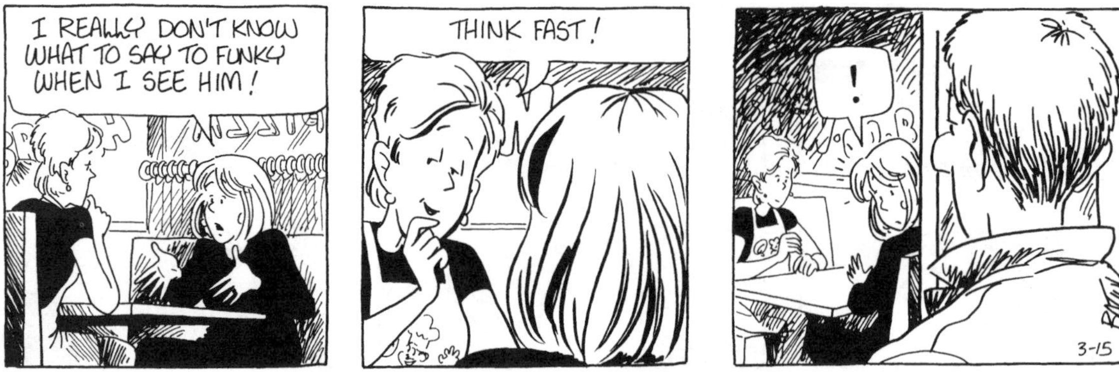
I REALLY DON'T KNOW WHAT TO SAY TO FUNKY WHEN I SEE HIM!
THINK FAST!
!
BATIUK
3-15

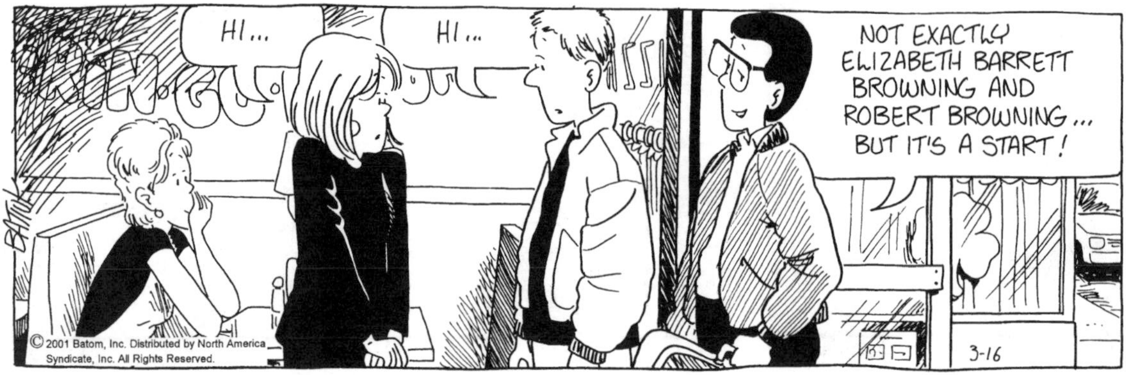
HI...
HI...
NOT EXACTLY ELIZABETH BARRETT BROWNING AND ROBERT BROWNING... BUT IT'S A START!
BATIUK
© 2001 Batom, Inc. Distributed by North America Syndicate, Inc. All Rights Reserved.
3-16

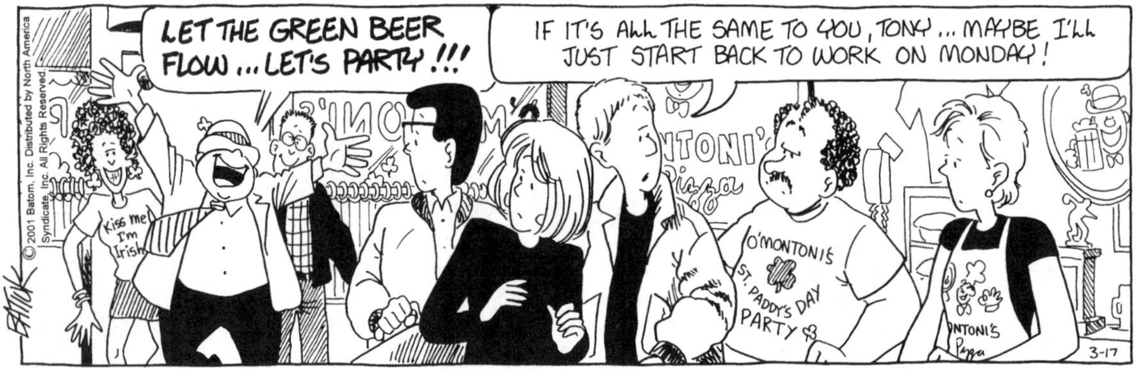
LET THE GREEN BEER FLOW... LET'S PARTY!!!
IF IT'S ALL THE SAME TO YOU, TONY... MAYBE I'LL JUST START BACK TO WORK ON MONDAY!
Kiss me! I'm Irish
O'MONTONI'S ST. PADDY'S DAY PARTY
ONTONI'S Pizza
© 2001 Batom, Inc. Distributed by North America Syndicate, Inc. All Rights Reserved.
BATIUK
3-17

SO WHAT WAS IT LIKE AT THE RE...?
HOW DID THINGS GO IN NEW...?
YOU FIRST!
WHAT WERE THINGS LIKE FOR YOU AT THE REHAB CENTER?
I WAS BASICALLY MISERABLE, LONELY AND SCARED!
WHAT DO YOU KNOW... ME TOO!
3-18
BATIUK

MORNINGS AT THE REHABILITATION CENTER WERE DEVOTED TO INDIVIDUAL COUNSELING...

AND IN THE AFTERNOON WE'D HAVE THE GROUP THERAPY SESSIONS!

HOW DID IT GO?

3-19

WELL, I'M STILL AN ALCOHOLIC... BUT THE GROUP WAS CURED!

IT'S FUNNY... I KNOW HOW I FEEL ABOUT YOU INSIDE...

BUT I FALL APART WHEN IT COMES TO COMMUNICATING IT TO YOU!

MAYBE YOU COULD GET YOUR MONEY BACK FOR ALL OF THOSE COMMUNICATIONS COURSES YOU TOOK IN COLLEGE!

GOOD POINT!

3-20

AND EVERY WEEKEND I'LL EITHER FLY HOME OR YOU CAN FLY TO NEW YORK!

IF OTHER COUPLES CAN DO IT, WE CAN TOO... WE'LL HAVE A BI-COASTAL MARRIAGE...

3-21

THE EAST COAST AND THE NORTH COAST!

DO YOU THINK WE SHOULD SEE A MARRIAGE COUNSELOR?

MAYBE IF WE DID WE WOULDN'T FIGHT SO MUCH!

WE DON'T FIGHT THAT MUCH!

OH, COME ON... GIVE ME A BREAK!

WELL, HEY... YOU MAKE IT SOUND LIKE THAT'S ALL WE DO!

NO, YOU'RE RIGHT... SOMETIMES WE SUHK!

JUST SEEING EACH OTHER ON WEEKENDS WILL CERTAINLY MAKE THEM MORE EXCITING!

LIKE THEY SAY... ABSTINENCE MAKES THE HEART GROW FONDER!

3-23

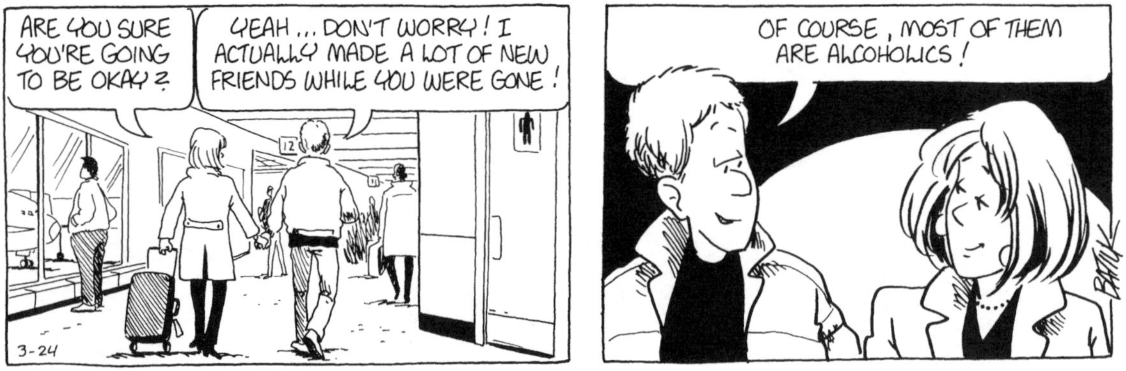
ARE YOU SURE YOU'RE GOING TO BE OKAY?
YEAH ... DON'T WORRY! I ACTUALLY MADE A LOT OF NEW FRIENDS WHILE YOU WERE GONE!
3-24
OF COURSE, MOST OF THEM ARE ALCOHOLICS!

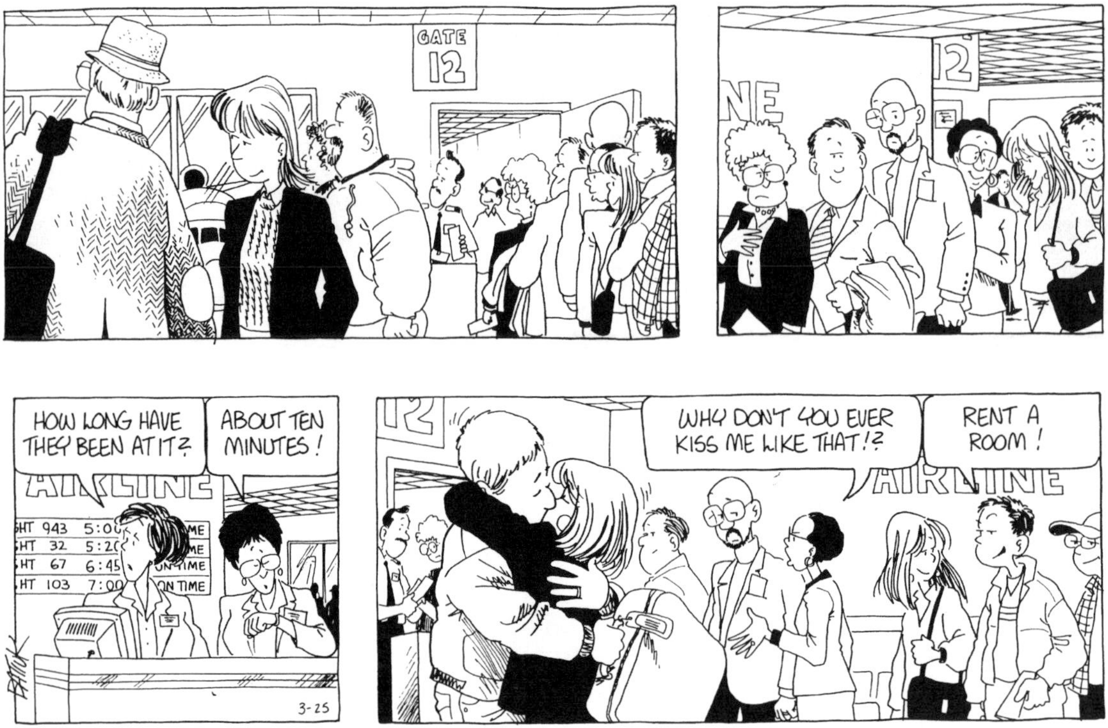
GATE 12
HOW LONG HAVE THEY BEEN AT IT?
ABOUT TEN MINUTES!
3-25
WHY DON'T YOU EVER KISS ME LIKE THAT!?
RENT A ROOM!

'LO !

WADE ... IT'S ME ... FUNKY !

REMEMBER HOW YOU SAID IF I EVER FELT THE URGE FOR A DRINK, I COULD CALL YOU ANYTIME, DAY OR NIGHT ?

SURE, FUNKY... ARE YOU HAVING A PROBLEM ?

ME? NO... I WAS JUST CHECKING OUT THE SYSTEM... CALL IT A DRY RUN !

ONE STEP AT A TIME

CUTE ... OKAY, PLAYTIME'S OVER, BUT REMEMBER...IF YOU REALLY DO NEED ME ...

GOTCHA !

4-22

THIS WAS REALLY A GREAT IDEA, LES!
I HAVEN'T PLAYED STRIP POKER WITH THE GUYS IN A LONG TIME!
EEEUUU!
THIS MAY BE A NONALCOHOLIC POKER PARTY IN DEFERENCE TO OUR FRIEND, FUNKY, HERE...
COACH
5-6
BUT THAT DOESN'T MEAN THAT WE CAN'T ENJOY OURSELVES!
SNIFF
BATIUK

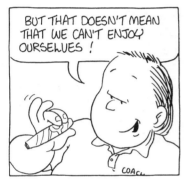

SOMETIMES THE GROUP ASPECTS OF AA TEND TO MAKE ME A LITTLE NERVOUS...

I GUESS I'VE NEVER REALLY TRUSTED THE JUDGMENT OF PEOPLE WHEN THEY START BEHAVING AS A GROUP!

IT'S PRETTY TYPICAL FOR ALCOHOLICS TO THINK OF THEMSELVES AS LONERS... PEOPLE WHO CAN DEAL WITH THINGS JUST FINE WITHOUT ANY HELP!

WHEN I WAS IN COLLEGE AND FOLKS WERE PROTESTING AGAINST THE MILITARY... I DIDN'T WANT ANY PART OF THE PROTESTORS OR THE MILITARY!

CHALK IT UP TO AN ALCOHOLIC'S AVERSION TO GROUP ACTIVITIES I GUESS!

7-22

I KNOW... I DON'T EVEN LIKE DOUBLES TENNIS!

THERE YOU GO!

BATIUK

I ASSUME YOU'VE DONE YOUR HOMEWORK AND ARE ALL SET FOR A DISCUSSION OF THE THIRD STEP...

ABOUT TURNING YOUR WILL AND LIFE OVER TO A HIGHER POWER!

YEAH... BUT SOMEHOW IT'S JUST NOT THAT SIMPLE FOR ME!

I MEAN, MY LIFE ISN'T A 'B.C.' COMIC STRIP!

IT WOULD PROBABLY HELP IF YOU'D START FOCUSING ON THE REST OF THE KNOWN UNIVERSE RATHER THAN ONLY ON THE FUNKYVERSE!

10-9

YOU NEED TO EXPAND A LITTLE ON YOUR FUNKYTHEISTIC WORLD VIEW!

HEY... DON'T PUT DOWN MY HOBBIES!

I LISTENED TO ELVIS PRESLEY'S 'LOVE ME TENDER' LIKE YOU SUGGESTED... AND THE PERFORMANCE IS TRANSCENDENT IN ITS SIMPLICITY AND BEAUTY! THAT'S SOMETHING I CAN BELIEVE IN!

WHAT ABOUT THE IDEA OF LOVE ITSELF?

I BELIEVE IN THAT TOO!

10-10

AND YET NONE OF THE THINGS YOU BELIEVE CAN BE MEASURED BY SCIENTIFIC INSTRUMENTS!

HOLD IT... I THINK I SEE WHERE THIS IS GOING...

 I ALSO READ BEN BOVA'S 'RETURN TO MARS' AND I THINK I UNDERSTAND WHAT YOU WANTED ME TO FIND THERE AS WELL...

 HE WRITES ABOUT A SPIRIT, A LIFE FORCE, A COLLECTIVE UNCONSCIOUS... AND HOW UNTIL WE ALLOW OURSELVES TO BECOME A PART OF THAT... WE CAN NEVER REALLY OWN OUR DREAMS AND AMBITIONS!

 ALTHOUGH, FRANKLY, I THINK IT WOULD BE EASIER IF LIFE JUST CAME WITH AN OWNER'S MANUAL!

WHAT ABOUT 'THE ELEGANT UNIVERSE' BY BRIAN GREENE... DID YOU FIND ANYTHING THERE?

AS A MATTER OF FACT... I DID WRITE SOME THINGS DOWN!

 'THE STUFF OF ALL MATTER AND ALL FORMS IS THE SAME... EACH ELEMENTARY PARTICLE IS COMPOSED OF A SINGLE STRING... ALL STRINGS ARE ABSOLUTELY IDENTICAL... DIFFERENCES ARISE BECAUSE PARTICLES HAVE DIFFERENT VIBRATION PATTERNS... DIFFERENT PARTICLES ARE REALLY DIFFERENT NOTES ON A FUNDAMENTAL STRING!'

I'D SAY YOU GOT IT!

WHOA... I JUST SAID I WROTE IT DOWN... I NEVER SAID I GOT IT!

10-12

I UNDERSTAND WHAT YOU'RE SAYING, WADE... ABOUT HAVING FAITH IN SOMETHING BEYOND OURSELVES...

10-13

BUT I GUESS I'M STILL STRUGGLING TO WRAP MY HEAD AROUND THE IDEA!

I KNOW, IT'S LIKE TRYING TO HOLD WATER IN YOUR HAND... YOU CAN ONLY DO IT IF YOU CUP YOUR HAND LOOSELY...

THE MINUTE YOU SQUEEZE TOO HARD... THE WATER RUNS OUT...

LIKE IDEAS RUNNING OUT OF MY BRAIN!

A couple of months later...

NO CHAMPAGNE FOR ME, TONY... JUST IN CASE I'M PREGNANT!

HOLD IT, TONY... I'LL TAKE LISA'S!

YOU GUYS SHOULDN'T BE HERE!

HEY, WE COULDN'T LET YOU SPEND NEW YEAR'S DAY ALONE HERE CLEANING UP!

BESIDES, IT SURE BEATS BEING HOME WATCHING 'IT'S A WONDERFUL LIFE' FOR THE UMPTEENTH TIME!

WHERE'S FUNKY... DIDN'T HE COME WITH YOU?

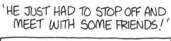

HE'LL BE ALONG SHORTLY!

'HE JUST HAD TO STOP OFF AND MEET WITH SOME FRIENDS!'

HI, MY NAME'S ALLAN AND I'M AN ALCOHOLIC!

HI, MY NAME'S FUNKY AND I'M AN ALCOHOLIC!

HI, FUNKY!

YOU KNOW, FUNKY... YOU'VE BEEN COMING TO THIS AA MEETING FOR ALMOST A YEAR NOW! ISN'T IT ABOUT TIME YOU TOLD US YOUR REAL NAME?

THIS PAST NEW YEAR'S EVE I TOASTED IN THE NEW YEAR WITH A GLASS OF GINGER ALE, AND YOU KNOW WHAT...?

THE NEW YEAR CAME IN RIGHT ON TIME JUST THE SAME!

ONE NEW YEAR'S EVE I WAS SO DRUNK THAT I GOT A BAG OF CHARCOAL BRIQUETS FROM THE GARAGE AND STARTED FILLING IN THE POTHOLES IN THE STREET!

THIS YEAR I HAD A CUP OF COFFEE AND LEFT THE STREET REPAIRS UP TO THE CITY!

HOW DO YOU THINK CINDY TOOK THE NEWS THAT I'M PREGNANT?

FINE!

YOU DIDN'T NOTICE ANY KIND OF SUBTLE UNDERCURRENT THERE?

NOPE... SHE SAID CONGRATULATIONS AND THAT WAS THAT!

IN SOME WAYS... LIFE IS SO SIMPLE FOR YOU!

HE'S PROBABLY GOING TO ASK ME WHAT I THINK ABOUT LES AND LISA HAVING A BABY!

SO TELL ME, CIN... WHAT DO YOU THINK ABOUT LES AND LISA HAVING A BABY?

IT'S SO SIMPLE FOR GUYS!

I THINK LES AND LISA ARE REALLY EXCITED ABOUT HER PREGNANCY!

I KNOW THAT'S HOW _THEY_ FEEL...

BUT I WANTED TO KNOW HOW _YOU_ FEEL!

DO YOU EVER THINK ABOUT US... YOU KNOW... HAVING A BABY?

SOMETIMES...

ACTUALLY... THAT'S THE LAST THING THAT I NEED TO THINK ABOUT RIGHT NOW!

I THINK SHE'S READY!

WHEN FUNKY WAS TALKING ABOUT US HAVING A BABY... HE HAD TO SENSE HOW UPTIGHT AND NERVOUS I WAS!

I DON'T THINK I'VE EVER SEEN CINDY THIS RELAXED AND CONTENT BEFORE!

CLICK!

'HE SHALL MARRY YOU AS A JOINER JOINS A FAULTY WAINSCOT... AND ONE OF YOU SHALL PROVE A SHRUNK PANEL AND WARP.'

I DON'T SEE HOW HAVING ONE IS REALLY GOING TO HURT!

DO YOU HONESTLY THINK THAT YOU COULD STOP AT JUST ONE, FUNKY?

3-17

LOOSEN UP, TONY... WHAT DIFFERENCE IS ONE LITTLE ONE GOING TO MAKE?

BESIDES, IT'S ST. PATRICK'S DAY AND I WANT TO CELEBRATE IN THE TRADITIONAL WAY, LIKE EVERYONE ELSE!

I'M SORRY ... BUT I DON'T KNOW IF WE'LL HAVE ENOUGH OF THESE SPECIAL IRISH CORNED BEEF AND CABBAGE PIZZAS TO GO AROUND FOR OUR CUSTOMERS!

DO YOU KNOW WHAT TIME IT IS?

AHHHH!!

BATIUK

4-22

OF COURSE I KNOW WHAT TIME IT IS!!

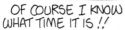

4-23

DO YOU THINK I'D BE TRYING TO SNEAK IN QUIETLY IF I DIDN'T KNOW IT WAS LATE AND THAT YOU MIGHT BE IN BED!?

HOW CONSIDERATE!

THAT WASN'T A COMPLIMENT!

THANK YOU!

SO I GUESSED!

LOOK, FUNKY... I'M SORRY I GOT IN SO LATE...

I TRIED CALLING... IF YOU WERE HERE, WHY DIDN'T YOU ANSWER?

BECAUSE I WAS AFRAID OF WHAT I MIGHT SAY!

4-24

I'M BEGINNING TO SEE WHY YOU DIDN'T HAVE MORE FRIENDS IN HIGH SCHOOL!

BATIUK

THIS ISN'T ABOUT MY GETTING HOME LATE... IT'S SOMETHING ELSE, ISN'T IT?

FINE! IF YOU DON'T WANT TO TALK I'M GOING TO...

YOUR AGENT SENT A COPY OF YOUR NEW CONTRACT HERE TO THE HOUSE!

TASSELLS!

AFTER OUR TALK THE OTHER NIGHT ABOUT STARTING A FAMILY... I JUST ASSUMED YOU'D BE COMING BACK FROM NEW YORK WHEN YOUR CONTRACT WAS UP...

WHY DIDN'T YOU TELL ME YOU'D SIGNED A NEW DEAL...

AND THAT YOU HAD NO PLANS TO COME HOME?

THIS IS WHY I KEEP PROMISING MYSELF I'M NEVER GOING TO TELL ANOTHER LIE!

YOU CAN START NOW BY TELLING THE TRUTH!

I'LL TRY... BUT I'M NOT VERY GOOD AT IT!

I KNOW WHAT YOU'RE PROBABLY THINKING RIGHT NOW...

AND I CAN'T SAY THAT I REALLY BLAME YOU!

IT'S TRUE THAT I SIGNED A NEW CONTRACT TO REMAIN WITH THE NETWORK IN NEW YORK...

BUT BEFORE I TRY TO EXPLAIN WHY I DIDN'T TELL YOU ABOUT THAT...

4-28

I'D JUST LIKE TO ASK ONE FAVOR...

WHEN ALL IS SAID AND DONE... TRY TO REMEMBER ME WHEN I WAS AT MY BEST!

I'D FULLY INTENDED TO COME HOME AFTER A YEAR...

' BUT WHEN SEPTEMBER 11TH HAPPENED... I SUDDENLY REALIZED...'

4-29

THAT NEW YORK CITY HAD BECOME MY HOME!

NOT ONLY DID I REALIZE THAT NEW YORK CITY HAD BECOME HOME TO ME...

BUT I ALSO REALIZED THAT AS MUCH AS I LOVE YOU... I ALSO LOVE BEING IN THE SPOTLIGHT ON THE BIGGEST STAGE IN THE WORLD...

4-30

SO WHEN I WAS OFFERED A NEW CONTRACT... I SIGNED IT!

I KNOW I WAS WRONG NOT TO TELL YOU RIGHT AWAY ABOUT THE CONTRACT...

I KNEW YOU'D BE UPSET AND I KEPT WAITING FOR THE RIGHT TIME TO TELL YOU... AND THE LONGER I WAITED THE HARDER IT BECAME...

5-1

UNTIL AT ONE POINT... NOT SAYING ANYTHING SUDDENLY BECAME EASY!

I KNOW HOW MUCH YOU WANT US TO SETTLE DOWN HERE IN WESTVIEW... HAVE LOTS OF KIDS...

BUT I'M NOT READY FOR THAT!

5-2

WE'RE ALL GOING TO DIE SOMEDAY... BUT I DON'T WANT TO BE BURIED WHILE I'M STILL ALIVE!

YOU KNOW, CINDY... YOU HAVEN'T CHANGED SINCE HIGH SCHOOL WHEN YOU WERE THE SCHOOL'S MOST POPULAR GIRL!

YOU STILL WANT EVERYBODY TO WANT YOU... BUT YOU DON'T WANT ANYONE TO NEED YOU!

I GUESS THIS IS WHERE I'M SUPPOSED TO BEAT MYSELF UP FOR ALL OF MY PAST SINS!

GO FOR IT!

5-3

JUST ONE QUESTION, CINDY... DID YOU EVER REALLY PLAN TO COME BACK FROM NEW YORK?

I CAN'T BELIEVE YOU'D ASK THAT!

I CAN'T BELIEVE YOU DIDN'T TELL ME ABOUT ALL OF THIS!

I CAN'T BELIEVE WE'RE DOING THIS!

5-4

COME ON, FUNKY...
STOP ME !
CINDY... WAIT !
5-5

YES
I'M GOING TO SEE A LAWYER TOMORROW... MAYBE YOU SHOULD TOO !
FINE ! AT LEAST WE'LL STILL BE IN TOUCH !
SLAM!

ARE YOU SURE YOU DON'T WANT SOME HELP CLOSING UP, FUNKY?

5-6

THANKS, RACHEL... I'LL BE FINE!

HOW ABOUT IF YOU LET ME SHIFT THE GEARS WHILE YOU DRIVE?

THIS IS MY DAD'S CAR... IF CINDY RUINS THE TRANSMISSION, HE'LL KILL ME!

OKAY!

5-7

DO YOU THINK WE HURT THE CAR BY DRIVING HOME WITH THE PARKING BRAKE ON?

NAW...

5-8

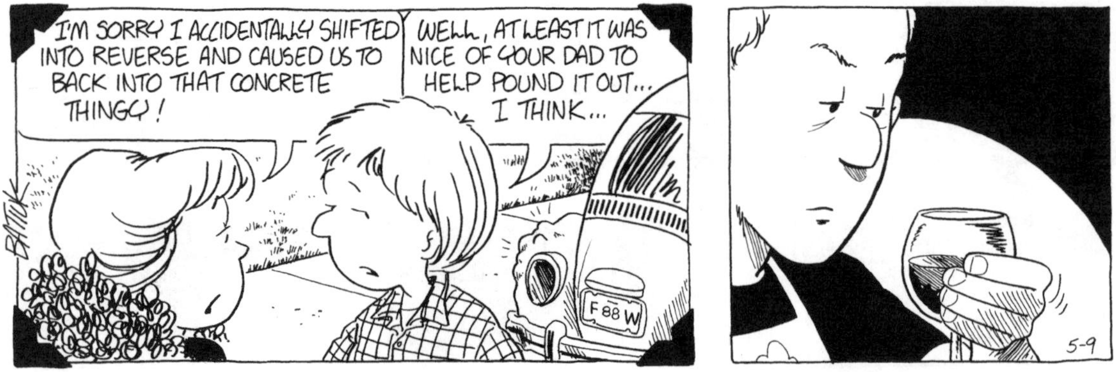
I'M SORRY I ACCIDENTALLY SHIFTED INTO REVERSE AND CAUSED US TO BACK INTO THAT CONCRETE THINGY!
WELL, AT LEAST IT WAS NICE OF YOUR DAD TO HELP POUND IT OUT... I THINK...
F 88 W
5-9

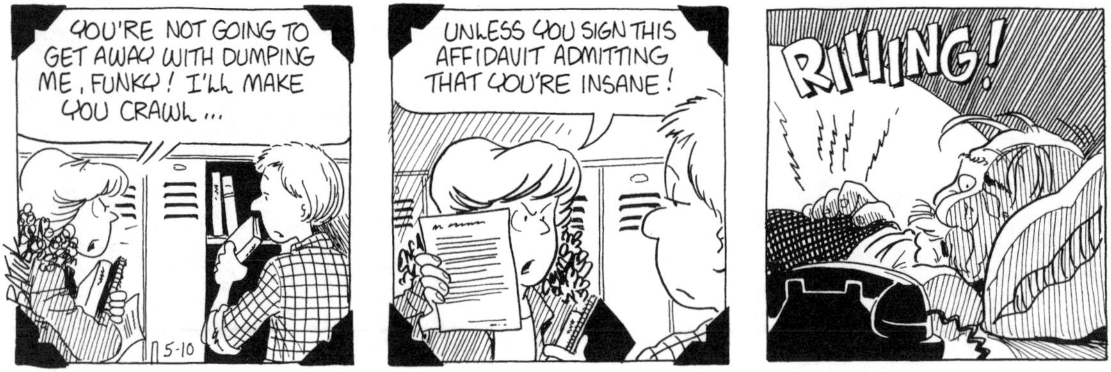
YOU'RE NOT GOING TO GET AWAY WITH DUMPING ME, FUNKY! I'LL MAKE YOU CRAWL...
5-10
UNLESS YOU SIGN THIS AFFIDAVIT ADMITTING THAT YOU'RE INSANE!
RIIIING!

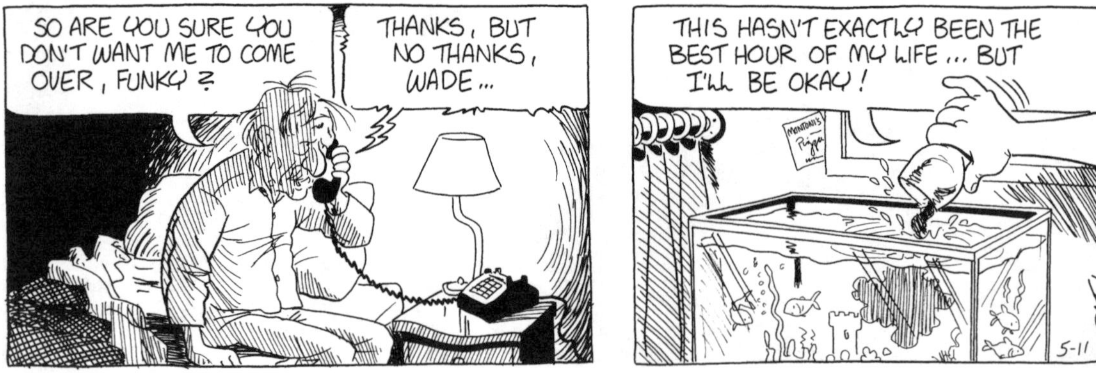
SO ARE YOU SURE YOU DON'T WANT ME TO COME OVER, FUNKY?
THANKS, BUT NO THANKS, WADE...
THIS HASN'T EXACTLY BEEN THE BEST HOUR OF MY LIFE... BUT I'LL BE OKAY!
5-11

CINDY! HAVE YOU COME BACK TO PICK UP THE PIECES?

I JUST CAME BACK TO PICK UP SOME THINGS FROM THE HOUSE!

5-20

LET'S FACE IT, CIN ... WE REALLY TRIED ... BUT IT JUST WASN'T MEANT TO BE!

I MEAN ... WHO'D HAVE THOUGHT THAT WESTVIEW'S MOST POPULAR GIRL WOULD END UP WITH THE GUY WITH THE GOOFIEST NAME IN THE SCHOOL?

YEAH, WHO'D HAVE THOUGHT ... HERE ARE MY KEYS TO THE HOUSE!

5-21

LOOK, I KNOW THIS ISN'T GOING TO BE EASY FOR EITHER OF US...

BUT THERE'S NO REASON WHY WE CAN'T BE ADULTS ABOUT IT!

5-22

TOO BAD WE DIDN'T THINK OF THAT SOONER!

YOU'RE PROBABLY RIGHT...

5-23

WE'RE BOTH A LITTLE TOO SCREWED UP TO MAKE THIS WORK!

MAYBE ONLY PERFECT PEOPLE SHOULD BE ALLOWED TO FALL IN LOVE!

WHO'D HAVE THOUGHT THAT WESTVIEW'S MOST POPULAR GIRL WOULD END UP WITH THE GUY WITH THE GOOFIEST NAME IN THE SCHOOL?

I DID!

5-24

'... JUST CAME BACK TO PICK UP A FEW THINGS FROM THE HOUSE!'

5-25

SO CINDY TOOK EVERYTHING, HUH?
TYPICAL... CINDY ALWAYS GETS WHAT SHE WANTS!
I'VE BEEN SLEEPING ON THE FLOOR WHILE CINDY'S LIVING THE GLAMOROUS LIFE IN NEW YORK CITY!
AT LEAST NOW I CAN SIT IN COMFORT WHILE I WATCH TV!
6-9

One month later...

I KNOW THAT THINGS AREN'T GOING TOO WELL BETWEEN YOU AND CINDY... BUT LISA CERTAINLY APPRECIATED CINDY'S HAVING THAT BABY SHOWER!

7-15

WELL, CINDY'S JUST FULL OF SURPRISES... SHE LEFT A LITTLE PRESENT FOR ME TOO!

DIVORCE PAPERS!?

IT'S NOT A CANDYGRAM!

CINDY IS FILING FOR A DIVORCE, AND IT LOOKS LIKE THINGS ARE GOING TO GET UGLY!

SHE WANTS PART OWNERSHIP OF MONTONI'S!?

7-16

WAIT TILL YOU GET TO THE PART ABOUT VISITATION RIGHTS FOR OUR CAT 'ANCHOVY'!

HAVE YOU TRIED TALKING WITH CINDY ABOUT ALL OF THIS?

OH, YEAH... MY STOBEX AND I GOT INTO A CLASSIC BLOWOUT WITH ALL THE TRIMMINGS!

7-17

STOBEX?

SOON-TO-BE EX!

THE PROBLEM IN TRYING TO REASON WITH CINDY IS THAT CINDY ALWAYS THINKS SHE'S RIGHT!

I CAN'T HELP YOU THERE... LISA ALWAYS IS RIGHT!

7-18

I STILL CAN'T BELIEVE THAT YOU AND CINDY ARE DIVORCING, FUNKY!

YOU BOTH SEEMED SO PERFECT TOGETHER!

IT WAS ALL A FACADE...

AND BENEATH THE FACADE WAS A UNIVERSE OF FEAR AND GALAXIES OF SELF-DOUBT!

7-19

WHATEVER YOU DO, FUNKY... DON'T GO BEATING YOURSELF UP OVER ALL OF THIS!

I DON'T HAVE TO...

I'VE GOT CINDY FOR THAT!

7-20

BEING MARRIED TO CINDY MEANT CONSTANTLY PUTTING OUT BRUSHFIRES...

AND DIFFUSING BOMBS THAT WERE ABOUT TO GO OFF!

WHENEVER I THINK ABOUT HOW MY MARRIAGE TO CINDY FELL APART... I'M REMINDED OF THIS AUTO REPAIR MANUAL THAT MY UNCLE USED TO HAVE IN HIS GARAGE...

EVERY SECTION IN THE MANUAL WAS WELL WORN AND COVERED WITH GREASY FINGERPRINTS EXCEPT FOR ONE...

THE ONE ON PREVENTIVE MAINTENANCE!

JUST REMEMBER... I'M HERE IF YOU NEED TO TALK!

YOU'RE ON THE SPEED DIAL, WADE!

A few months later...

THE MOST IMPORTANT THING IN WORKING THROUGH THE TWELVE STEPS...

IS NOT TO PLAY GAMES WITH YOURSELF... BECAUSE GAMES ARE ALWAYS PLAYED UNTIL SOMEONE LOSES.

REMEMBER, FUNKY... ENJOY LIFE'S JOURNEY ONE DAY AT A TIME.

EVEN THOUGH IT'S ONLY A ONE-WAY TICKET?

10-27

YES... EVEN THOUGH IT'S ONLY A ONE-WAY TICKET.

THAT'S GOING TO MAKE IT PRETTY TOUGH TO STAY LOOSE.

TRY.

CINDY WAS HERE?

MON 12-16

YEAH, SHE CAME BY TO PICK UP THE KEYS TO THE HOUSE SO SHE COULD GO PICK UP SOME OF HER STUFF!

12-16

I'M SURPRISED SHE DIDN'T SEND HER LAWYERS TO DO IT!

I'D FORGOTTEN ALL ABOUT THIS BOX OF CHRISTMAS PHOTOS!

12-17

HMMM... THIS MUST BE FROM MY FRESHMAN YEAR IN HIGH SCHOOL... I REMEMBER THAT SWEATER MY FOLKS GOT ME...

HOW NICE... I KNOW JUST WHAT I CAN EXCHANGE IT FOR!

I'D FORGOTTEN ALL ABOUT THAT TOY MALL THAT MY FOLKS GOT FOR ME WHEN I WAS TEN!

Christmas Photos 12-18

THIS IS SO REALISTIC... SEE? THERE ARE EVEN LITTLE FRENCH FRIES ON THE FLOOR OF THE FOOD COURT!

AND LOOK... YOU CAN PUT THESE PARTITIONS INTO THE CINEMAS AND MAKE THEM EVEN SMALLER!

MERRY CHRISTMAS, CINDY!

MERRY CHRISTMAS, FUNKY....

12-19

HERE'S THE KEY TO THE HOUSE...

12-20

LISTEN... ARE YOU GOING TO BE...?

YEAH! LOOK... NOT TO RUIN THE MOMENT OR ANYTHING...

BUT I'VE GOT THINGS I HAVE TO GET TO IN THE BACK!

CINDY...I'M GLAD I CAUGHT YOU! I WANTED TO GIVE YOU SOME BABY PICTURES OF SUMMER!

12-21

IT'S NICE THAT YOU CAME BACK FOR CRAZY'S WEDDING!

WELL, IT'S NICE TO SEE SOMEONE HEADED OFF ON THE ROAD TO WEDDED BLISS...

ESPECIALLY WHEN YOUR OWN IS CLOSED FOR DEMOLITION!

Several months later...

SO WHAT DID YOU THINK OF THE REUNION, LES?

IT WAS OKAY... ALTHOUGH I WAS A BIT SURPRISED WHEN I FIRST WALKED IN AND SAW ALL OF THOSE OLDER PEOPLE STANDING AROUND.

TRUE... I MUST SAY, THOUGH, THAT CINDY LOOKED FAIRLY BREATHTAKING.

8-4

ACCORDING TO FUNKY... THAT'S BECAUSE SHE SUCKS THE AIR OUT OF ANY ROOM THAT SHE'S IN.

YOU HAVE TO WONDER IF IT WAS MAINLY CINDY'S LOOKS THAT GOT HER THAT ANCHOR JOB IN NEW YORK CITY.

HARD TO SAY... CINDY'S NO DUMMY...

8-5

BUT I GUESS WE'LL HAVE TO WAIT TILL HER LOOKS FADE TO REALLY SEE IF SHE'S GOT ANYTHING UNDER THE HOOD.

SO CINDY AND FUNKY ARE GETTING TOGETHER WITH THEIR LAWYERS TODAY?

YEAH... APPARENTLY CINDY'S LAWYERS HAVE FILED A MOTION TO HAVE ALL OF FUNKY'S BANK ACCOUNTS FROZEN.

IT LOOKS LIKE FUNKY WILL BE FORCED TO PAY HIS ATTORNEY'S WITH COLD HARD CASH.

8-6

JUST TO CONFIRM A FEW THINGS HERE... THERE ARE NO CHILDREN INVOLVED HERE, IS THAT CORRECT?

NO... NO CHILDREN...

UNLESS YOU COUNT THE TWO OF US.

8-7

THAT TAKES CARE OF ALMOST ALL OF THE PROPERTY, WITH THE EXCEPTION OF THE PIZZA RESTAURANT MONTONI'S.

WE FEEL THAT CINDY IS ENTITLED TO ONE HALF OF THE...

NO...

BUT WE WENT OVER THESE THINGS AND...

I MEAN, NO... I DON'T WANT TO DO THIS.

8-8

FUNKY... HOW ABOUT IF YOU AND I GO FIND A PLACE WHERE WE CAN TALK.

8-9

AS YOUR ATTORNEY, I HAVE TO ADVISE YOU THAT IT ISN'T...

AS THE PERSON PAYING THE BILLS, I'D LIKE TO ADVISE YOU THAT I'LL DO WHATEVER I PLEASE.

I THOUGHT YOU TWO WERE MEETING WITH THE LAWYERS.

8-11

WE WERE... IS LISA AROUND?

YEAH, SHE'S UPSTAIRS IN THE APARTMENT. WHY?

WE WANT TO GET A SECOND OPINION.

I'M NOT REALLY TRAINED IN DOMESTIC RELATIONS LAW...

BUT IF NEITHER OF YOU IS CONTESTING ANYTHING... I SUPPOSE I COULD PREPARE A SIMPLE DISSOLUTION AGREEMENT.

8-12

HOWEVER, I HAVE TO TELL YOU THAT HAVING ONLY ONE ATTORNEY HANDLING A DIVORCE ISN'T THE BEST WAY TO DO IT.

TRUST ME... WE TRIED THE BEST WAY AND IT DIDN'T WORK.

THANKS FOR HELPING US OUT, LISA.

ME TOO... YOU'RE A GOOD FRIEND.

MORONI'S PIZZA

8-13

IF I WAS A GOOD FRIEND, I'D BE TRYING TO MEDIATE THIS AND GET YOU TWO INTO MARRIAGE COUNSELING.

THE SHIP'S ALREADY HIT THE SAND ... WE JUST NEED TO BE RESCUED.

AS SOON AS LISA PREPARES ALL THE PAPERS... YOU'LL BE FREE TO PURSUE YOUR CAREER WITHOUT ANY REGRETS.

8-14

NOT EXACTLY...

I...   I'M...

YOU FIRST...

NOTHING.

YEAH, ME TOO.

8-15

HEY... WE GAVE IT THE OLD SCHOOL TRY, RIGHT?

RIGHT.

TOO BAD OUR SCHOOL MASCOT WAS A SCAPEGOAT.

8-16

87

Several months later...

BACK IN COLLEGE WHEN WE WERE CLEANING UP AFTER A PARTY LIKE THIS...

WE USED TO FINISH OFF WHATEVER WAS LEFT IN THE BOTTLES.

WE CALLED IT BAYONETTING THE WOUNDED.

WE MISSED YOU AT THE AA MEETING LAST WEEK, FUNKY.

HOW WAS ITALY?

WONDERFUL, WADE... BUT THEY SURE LIKE THEIR WINE OVER THERE.

AND...?

IT WAS NIP AND TUCK...

BUT I MANAGED TO AVOID TAKING A NIP.

WE'D WON THE MIDWEST PIZZA COMPETITION... WE WERE ON A PAID-FOR TRIP TO ITALY...

AND ALL I COULD THINK ABOUT WAS HAVING A DRINK... WHY IS THAT?

SOMETIMES SUCCESS COURTS DISASTER EVEN MORE THAN FAILURE DOES.

YOU'VE BEEN TRYING TO DESTROY YOURSELF ALL THESE YEARS... WHY WOULD YOU SUDDENLY BE NICE TO YOURSELF JUST BECAUSE THINGS START GOING WELL?

CHANGE OF PACE?

I GUESS I'M STILL ON HOLD WITH THAT SPIRITUAL AWAKENING PART OF THE DEAL, WADE.

LOOK UP AT THOSE STARS AND TELL ME WHAT YOU SEE.

AN AWFUL LOT OF BLACK IN BETWEEN THEM.

YOU REALLY SEE THE CUP AS HALF FULL, DON'T YOU?

ACTUALLY, I'D PREFER A GLASS.

YOU SEE, WADE... I LOOK OUT THERE AND SEE A UNIVERSE THAT'S A NON-DIRECTED, RANDOM THING...

COULD'VE BEEN SOMEWHERE ELSE...

BUT RIGHT NOW IT HAPPENS TO BE HERE.

AND I SAY, AMEN!

JUST FOR THE SAKE OF ARGUMENT, LET'S SAY THAT EVERYTHING, GOOD AND BAD AND IN BETWEEN, IS ALL MEANINGLESS TO THE COSMOS...

IT JUST DOESN'T CARE.

CAN'T WE STILL TAKE COMFORT FROM THE FACT THAT THERE'S THIS BIG, BEAUTIFUL UNIVERSE TO ADMIRE THAT CAN'T BE TWISTED FOR GOOD OR EVIL... IT'S JUST SIMPLY THERE?

WHATEVER FLOATS YOUR SKIFF, SKIPPER.

I GUESS TRYING TO FIGURE OUT THIS LIFE-AFTER-DEATH THING IS STILL GOING TO TAKE ME A WHILE, WADE.

ROME WASN'T BUILT IN A DAY.

EXACTLY... I'M STILL TRYING TO FIGURE OUT LIFE AFTER BIRTH.

4-17

YOU GO ON, LISA... I'LL TAKE CARE OF WHAT WE OWE.

YOU SURE?

5-6

HEY, IT'S A DIRTY JOB... BUT THE GROUP'S TREASURER HAS TO DO IT.

BESIDES... IT'LL GIVE ME A CHANCE TO BE ALONE WITH FUNKY.

YOU DON'T OWE ANYTHING FOR THE USE OF THE ROOM, HOLLY... IT'S ON THE HOUSE.

YOU SURE?

HE'S STILL LOOKING PRETTY GOOD.

5-7

ABSOLUTELY... IT'S THE LEAST WE CAN DO.

AND HE'S STILL PRETTY COOL.

THANKS AGAIN FOR LETTING OUR SUPPORT GROUP HAVE THE USE OF THE ROOM, FUNKY.

ANYTIME... JUST LET ME KNOW WHEN I CAN HELP OUT.

OKAY, THAT WAS NICE...NOW LEAVE.

SO...HOW DID THINGS FINALLY WORK OUT WITH YOU AND CINDY?

WHOA ...WHAT ARE YOU DOING?

AND SINCE OUR DIVORCE... I REALLY HAVEN'T HAD MUCH CONTACT WITH CINDY.

I'M SORRY.

LIKE HECK YOU ARE.

DON'T BE... WE WEREN'T IN A HAPPY PLACE...

IT WAS BASICALLY AN EXIT LOOKING FOR A SCENE.

I KNOW THE FEELING.

LEAVE NOW, GIRL...BEFORE YOU DO SOMETHING REALLY STUPID.

MY HUSBAND ACTUALLY LEFT ME FOR SOMEONE HE MET ON THE INTERNET...

LEAVING ME TO DEAL WITH A BABY AND CHEMO TREATMENTS.

THAT'S RIGHT...

TELL HIM YOUR LIFE STORY, WHY DON'T YOU?

THEY SAY MARRIAGE IS FOR A LIFETIME.

AND THAT'S ABOUT HOW LONG IT'S GOING TO TAKE TO GET OVER IT...HEH, HEH.

YOU SOUND LIKE THE AFLAC DUCK WHEN YOU LAUGH.

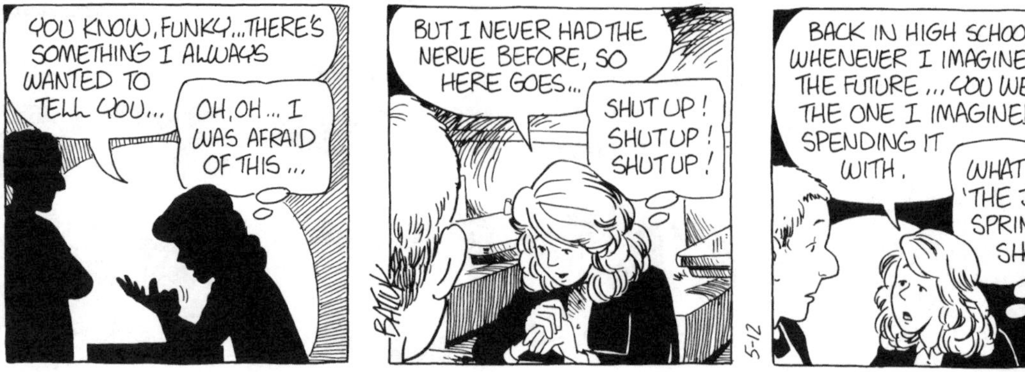
YOU KNOW, FUNKY...THERE'S SOMETHING I ALWAYS WANTED TO TELL YOU...
OH, OH... I WAS AFRAID OF THIS...
BUT I NEVER HAD THE NERVE BEFORE, SO HERE GOES...
SHUT UP! SHUT UP! SHUT UP!
BACK IN HIGH SCHOOL, WHENEVER I IMAGINED THE FUTURE... YOU WERE THE ONE I IMAGINED SPENDING IT WITH.
WHAT IS THIS... 'THE JERRY SPRINGER SHOW'?
5-12

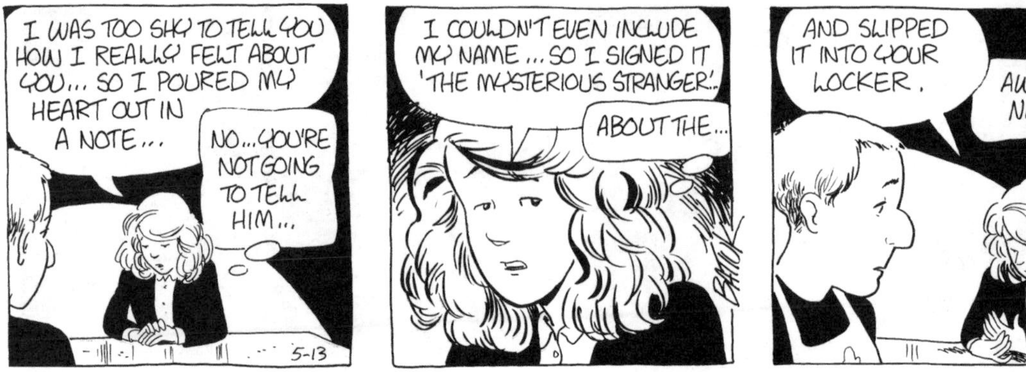
I WAS TOO SHY TO TELL YOU HOW I REALLY FELT ABOUT YOU... SO I POURED MY HEART OUT IN A NOTE...
NO...YOU'RE NOT GOING TO TELL HIM...
5-13
I COULDN'T EVEN INCLUDE MY NAME... SO I SIGNED IT 'THE MYSTERIOUS STRANGER'..
ABOUT THE...
AND SLIPPED IT INTO YOUR LOCKER.
AWWW NUTS.

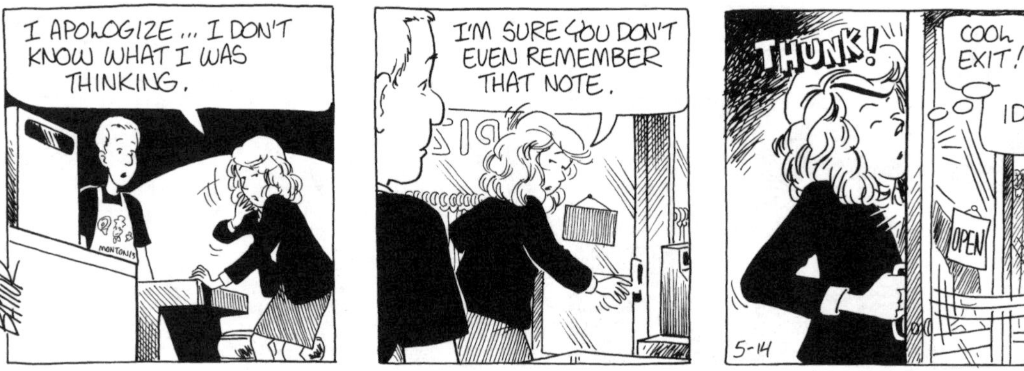
I APOLOGIZE... I DON'T KNOW WHAT I WAS THINKING.
I'M SURE YOU DON'T EVEN REMEMBER THAT NOTE.
THUNK!
COOL EXIT!
IDIOT!
OPEN
5-14

Your secret admirer, the Mysterious Stranger

HOLLY... I WANTED TO SEE IF YOU HAD ANY INFORMATION ON AN OLD CLASSMATE...

CINDY... FUNKY...

I GUESS THAT TAKES CARE OF THE INTRODUCTIONS.

HEY... HEY...

I'LL TELL YOU WHAT...YOU TWO JUST KEEP ON CHATTING... I'LL BE RIGHT BACK...

THAT SEEMED KIND OF AWKWARD BACK THERE WITH CINDY...

I'M SORRY I INVITED YOU TO THE GRADUATION.

ACTUALLY, I WAS IMPRESSED...

I THOUGHT CINDY DID A GREAT JOB WITH THE COMMENCEMENT ADDRESS.

NOW I'M REALLY SORRY.

'GLORY' SHOWED UP FOR ONE OF OUR REHEARSALS...

6-10

AND SHE COULD ACTUALLY STILL FIT INTO HER OLD MAJORETTE UNIFORM...

SO FOR REASONS OF ALUMNI BAND MORALE ... WE ASKED HER NOT TO COME BACK.

I'M GOING TO A MAJORETTE CLINIC NEXT WEEK, FUNKY.

6-11

GOOD LUCK, HOLLY... I KNOW YOU CAN KICK IT.

YOU WERE QUITE THE WIT BACK IN HIGH SCHOOL.

WELL, HALF ANYWAY...

THERE'S SOMETHING I'VE ALWAYS WONDERED ABOUT...

EXACTLY WHAT IS 'FUNKY' SHORT FOR, ANYWAY?

6-12

FUNNNNNNKY!

WHY AM I DOING THIS? WHY AM I GETTING A NEW HAIRSTYLE?

7-12

IS IT BECAUSE FUNKY'S EX TURNED UP AT THE GRADUATION CEREMONY LOOKING HOTTER THAN HIGH SCHOOL? IF THAT'S POSSIBLE...

OR MAYBE I'M JUST TRYING TO INTRODUCE SOME MYSTERY... LIKE WHY AM I DOING THIS?

I'D BETTER GET RID OF ANY TRACES OF OLD ROMANCES BEFORE FUNKY ARRIVES.

7-13

IT'S NOT EXACTLY LIKE THERE'S BEEN A REVOLVING DOOR ON THE PLACE...

BUT THE EX-HUSBAND AND THE EX-BOYFRIEND NEED TO GO IN THE EX-FILES.

LET'S SEE ... WHAT ELSE DO I NEED TO STASH BEFORE FUNKY GETS HERE?

I GUESS IT'S BEST TO FOLLOW THE BASIC RULE OF THUMB ...

AND GET RID OF ANYTHING I'D WANT OUT OF SIGHT IF MY PARENTS WERE COMING OVER.

7-14

HMMM ... DIET AND EXERCISE BOOKS.

7-15

IT'S BEST NOT TO LET A NEW BOYFRIEND SEE THESE.

WHY HAVE A BIG ARROW POINTING TO PROBLEM AREAS?

THERE ... I THINK THE PLACE IS SET FOR FUNKY'S ARRIVAL.

IT COULD PROBABLY BE A LITTLE CLEANER...

7-16

BUT HEY... HE'S A GUY.

I WANT HIM TO FEEL AT HOME.

FUNKY'S HERE... I THINK I'VE MANAGED TO HIDE EVERYTHING THAT COULD SCARE HIM OFF...

7-17

AND IF YOU SCARE HIM OFF, SWEETIE... THAT'S JUST TOO @#@ BAD.

I LIKE YOUR NEW HAIRDO, HOLLY.

THANKS... A LOT OF GUYS WOULDN'T EVEN HAVE NOTICED.

I THINK YOU'LL FIND THAT WE DIVORCED GUYS COME INSTALLED WITH EXTRA MEMORY AND UPGRADED AWARENESS.

7-19

AND YOU'VE GOT MY CELL PHONE NUMBER IN CASE YOU NEED TO REACH ME.

7-20

CUTE KID.

THE BABYSITTER?

NO... YOUR SON.

JUST CHECKING.

I'LL HAVE A GLASS OF WHITE WINE, PLEASE.

JUST WATER FOR ME.

7-21

I'M SORRY...

ME TOO...BUT I'M A FAITHFUL FOLLOWER OF BILL W.

SO YOU CAN'T TOUCH ALCOHOL...

TOUCHING IT... NO PROBLEM.

DRINKING IT... BIG PROBLEM.

HOW OLD IS YOUR SON CORY?

ALMOST TWO.

7-22

IT'S FUNNY... I ALWAYS PICTURED CINDY AND ME HAVING A LARGE FAMILY.

I GUESS I WASN'T AFRAID OF COMMITMENT.

MAYBE I SHOULD'VE BEEN.

BEEP! BEEP! BEEP!

HI, I JUST WANTED TO REMIND YOU THAT THIS IS A SCHOOL NIGHT FOR ME AND I HAVE TO BE HOME EARLY.

I SWEAR, JENNY...IF BABYSITTERS WEREN'T SO HARD TO FIND...

7-23

Approximately eight months later...

SO YOU DON'T RECOGNIZE THE GIRL THAT YOU TOOK TO YOUR SENIOR PROM?

GO TO THE HEAD OF THE CLASS.

VICKY!?

WOW...IT'S BEEN A LONG TIME...

AND BY THE WAY, YOU LOOK TERRIFIC.

YOU LOOK BETTER.

3-22

...AND SINCE I'LL BE WORKING OVERSEAS FOR THE NEXT FEW YEARS...

I THOUGHT I'D STOP BY HOME TO SEE SOME FRIENDS AND CATCH UP ON OLD TIMES BEFORE I LEAVE.

SOUNDS PERFECT... BUT WE'LL HAVE TO MAKE IT A BUSMAN'S HOLIDAY.

APPARENTLY TONY HAS RENTED MONTONI'S OUT FOR SOME KIND OF PRIVATE PARTY THIS AFTERNOON AND I WAS TOLD TO MAKE MYSELF SCARCE UNTIL ABOUT FIVE O'CLOCK.

3-23

AND REMEMBER THE TIME CINDY SUMMERS FELL ASLEEP IN THE TANNING BOOTH AND SHOWED UP AT THE PROM LOOKING LIKE A BEET?

3-24

I'VE NEVER SEEN YOU AT ANY OF THE CLASS REUNIONS, VICKY.

HOW COME?

LACK OF INTEREST, I SUPPOSE.

REUNIONS JUST SORT OF SEEMED LIKE HIGH SCHOOL WITH WEIGHT GAIN AND MONEY!

I'M SORRY TO HEAR ABOUT YOU AND CINDY...
WHAT WE NEED TO DO IS ORDER A COUPLE OF DRINKS AND TOAST TO BETTER DAYS...
I REALLY SHOULDN'T...
3-25
JUST FOR OLD TIMES' SAKE.
WELL, I GUESS ONE DRINK WON'T HURT.

ARE YOU SURE I CAN'T DROP YOU OFF SOMEPLACE, FUNKY?
NAW ... I'M JUSH FINE.
Bistro
3-26
MY CAR KNOWSH THE WAY HOME.

I PARKED IN FRONT OF MONTONI'S WISSSH NOOOO PROBLEM.
MONTONI'S
WHOA! WHO MOVED THE SCHIDWALK ?
I PROBABLY SHOULDN'T HAVE HAD THOSE DRINKS ... BUT ALL I HAVE TO DO IS GET INSIDE ...
PIZZ
3-27
AND NO ONE WILL BE THE WISER ...
www.kingfeatures.com
BATIUK
SURPRISE!!
MONTONI'S Pizza

SURPRISE!!

MONTONI'S Pizza

THIS ISH THE MOST FESTIVE INTERVENTION I'VE BEEN TO YET!

3-28

I JUST WENT TO LUNCE WITH AN OLD FRIEND...

AND WE HAD ONLY ONE DRINK...

AT A TIME...

3-29

SO WHO WAS THIS OLD FRIEND? JACK DANIEL'S?

3-30

NO... IT WASHH AN OLD GIRLFRIEND.

THIS JUST GETS BETTER AND BETTER.

SO AN OLD FLAME FROM HIGH SCHOOL SHOWS UP...

AND RATHER THAN ADMIT THAT YOU'RE AN ALCOHOLIC... YOU FELL OFF THE WAGON.

THAT'S NOT EXACTLY TRUE.

ACTUALLY, I FELL OFF THE SIDEWALK OUT FRONT.

I GUESS I REALLY RUINED EVERYTHING, DIDN'T I?

IT WASN'T YOUR FINEST HOUR.

I'D HAVE TO SAY THAT THIS YEAR...

APRIL FOOL'S DAY HAS BEEN SPONSORED BY FUNKY WINKERBEAN.

YOU'RE RIGHT, TONY...

I REALLY MADE A FOOL OF MYSELF.

HOLLY LEFT BEFORE I COULD EVEN TALK TO HER. HOW DID SHE TAKE IT?

SHE LEFT THIS FOR YOU...

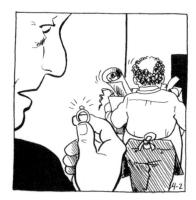

GOOD MORNING... IT'S NINE A.M. ...

I'M LIANE HANSEN AND YOU'RE LISTENING TO NPR'S WEEKEND EDITION.

JUST A REMINDER IN CASE YOU HAVEN'T ALREADY DONE SO...

@#%! WHAT THE @#% WAS I THINKING...?

DAYLIGHT SAVINGS TIME BEGINS TODAY...

I'VE REALLY SCREWED THINGS UP ROYALLY THIS TIME.

SO YOU'LL NEED TO TURN YOUR CLOCKS AHEAD ONE HOUR.

PERFECT... AN EXTRA HOUR OF DAYLIGHT.

WHY DIDN'T YOU CALL WHEN YOU WANTED TO HAVE THAT FIRST DRINK?

I DUNNO... I GUESS I THOUGHT I COULD DEAL WITH IT.

I THOUGHT THAT BY NOW I WAS TOUGH ENOUGH.

TOUGH GUY, HUH?

WE TEND TO BURY A LOT OF THOSE.

YOU COULD'VE KNOCKED ME OVER WITH A FEATHER WHEN YOU SHOWED UP LOADED AT YOUR BIRTHDAY PARTY.

YOU REALLY FOOLED ME.

I KNOW... AND I WAS THINKING...

MAYBE WHAT I NEED IS A MORE PERCEPTIVE SPONSOR.

CUTE.

ALL OF THESE WONDERFUL THINGS ARE HAPPENING IN YOUR LIFE...

AND YET DEEP INSIDE YOU DON'T FEEL AS IF YOU DESERVE IT.

YOU FEEL THAT IF PEOPLE KNEW WHAT YOU WERE REALLY LIKE... THEY WOULDN'T LIKE YOU.

YEAH...

IT'S THE CLASSIC IMPOSTER SYNDROME.

AS CHARLIE BROWN USED TO SAY...

THAT'S IT!!

SO WHERE DOES THIS IMPOSTER SYNDROME COME FROM ANYWAY?

OFTEN YOU'RE BORN INTO THIS LIFE PAYING FOR THE SINS OF SOMEBODY ELSE'S PAST.

IS THAT FROM BILL W. AND THE BIG BOOK?

NO, ACTUALLY IT'S FROM BRUCE SPRINGSTEEN AND 'ADAM RAISED A CAIN.' APPARENTLY THE GUY WAS DEEPER THAN HE LOOKED.

4-14

OKAY, SO HOW DO I LIGHTEN UP AND UNLOAD THESE 'SINS OF SOMEBODY ELSE'S PAST'?

YOU DON'T HAVE TO, BECAUSE THEY DON'T MATTER.

4-15

THE ONLY REAL SIN IS SELF-HATRED.

MEA CULPA... MEA CULPA... MEA CULPA...

SO I HAVE TO LEARN HOW NOT TO HATE MYSELF?

MAKES SENSE, DOESN'T IT?

4-16

WHY WOULD YOU DO SOMETHING NICE FOR SOMEONE YOU DIDN'T LIKE?

THAT'S WHY I FEEL SO BAD ABOUT THE MESS I'VE MADE OF THINGS WITH HOLLY.

I'D ALMOST STARTED TO LIKE MYSELF SINCE I FOUND HER.

Several months later...

HEY, TONY... CAN YOU HANDLE THINGS FOR A COUPLE OF HOURS WHILE I TAKE OFF?

WHAT'S THE NAME OF THIS PLACE?

WHAT'S MY NAME?

MONTONI'S.

TONY MONTONI.

11-29

YEAH... I THINK I CAN HANDLE THINGS FOR A COUPLE OF HOURS.

HI, THIS IS HOLLY... I CAN'T COME TO THE PHONE RIGHT NOW...

11-30

BUT YOU CAN LEAVE ME A MESSAGE AFTER THE LONG BEEP...

HI, HOLLY... I THOUGHT I'D TAKE A CHANCE THAT MAYBE YOU WERE IN.

YOU WERE TAKING A CHANCE ALL RIGHT!

12-1

A CHANCE THAT I MIGHT STRANGLE YOU!

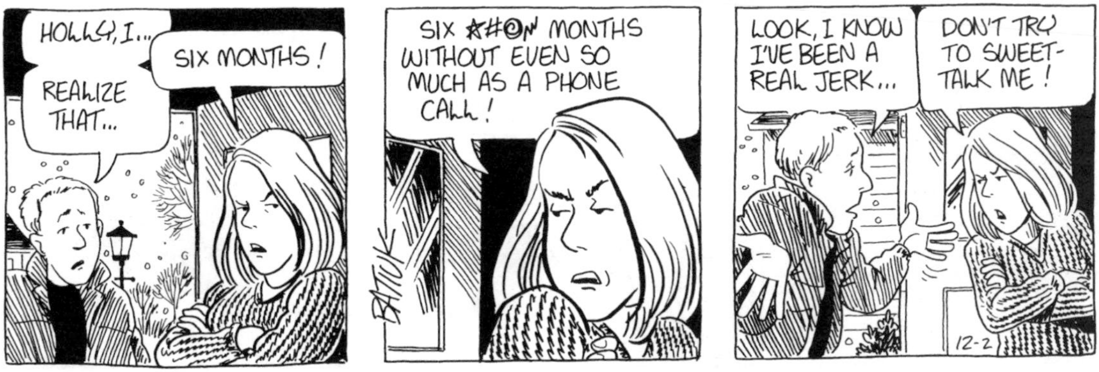
HOLLY, I...
REALIZE THAT...
SIX MONTHS!
SIX ☆#@~ MONTHS WITHOUT EVEN SO MUCH AS A PHONE CALL!
BATIUK
LOOK, I KNOW I'VE BEEN A REAL JERK...
DON'T TRY TO SWEET-TALK ME!
12-2

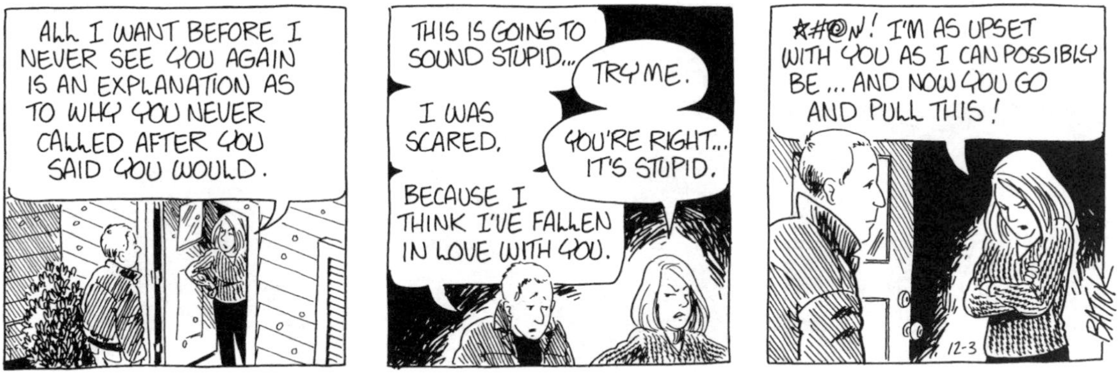
ALL I WANT BEFORE I NEVER SEE YOU AGAIN IS AN EXPLANATION AS TO WHY YOU NEVER CALLED AFTER YOU SAID YOU WOULD.
THIS IS GOING TO SOUND STUPID...
TRY ME.
I WAS SCARED.
YOU'RE RIGHT... IT'S STUPID.
BECAUSE I THINK I'VE FALLEN IN LOVE WITH YOU.
☆#@~! I'M AS UPSET WITH YOU AS I CAN POSSIBLY BE... AND NOW YOU GO AND PULL THIS!
12-3
BATIUK

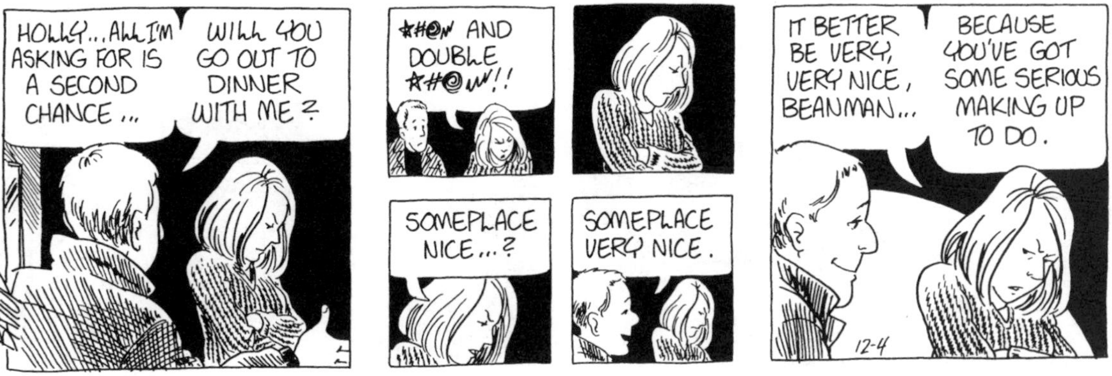
HOLLY... ALL I'M ASKING FOR IS A SECOND CHANCE...
WILL YOU GO OUT TO DINNER WITH ME?
BATIUK
☆#@~ AND DOUBLE ☆#@~!!
SOMEPLACE NICE...?
SOMEPLACE VERY NICE.
IT BETTER BE VERY, VERY NICE, BEANMAN...
BECAUSE YOU'VE GOT SOME SERIOUS MAKING UP TO DO.
12-4

SO... IS THIS A NICE PLACE?

YES, IT'S A VERY NICE PLACE.

LOOK... I'M SORRY ABOUT THE RANT, I...

FORGET ABOUT IT... ALTHOUGH I MUST ADMIT THAT I NEVER REALIZED WHAT A POTTY MOUTH YOU HAD.

I SUPPOSE WHEN YOU'VE BEEN THROUGH CANCER, CHEMO AND A DIVORCE... YOU TEND TO LOSE YOUR INHIBITIONS.

NO @!$☆#N!

12-27

LISTEN, HOLLY,... I'M THE ONE WHO OWES YOU AN APOLOGY.

I WAS NERVOUS ABOUT FALLING TOO FAST... AND AFRAID I'D GET MY HEART SHREDDED AGAIN...

12-28

BECAUSE SCOTCH TAPE AND CRAZY GLUE HAVE BEEN THE ONLY THINGS HOLDING IT TOGETHER SINCE MY MARRIAGE ENDED.

REGRET IS RESERVED FOR THE THINGS WE DIDN'T DO...

AND I DIDN'T WANT TO LET WHAT WE MAY HAVE SLIP AWAY.

I'M ONLY SORRY THAT I DIDN'T REALIZE IT SOONER.

'S OKAY... I STAYED IN LOVE WITH YOU JUST IN CASE.

12-29

YOU KNOW... IT IS NEW YEAR'S EVE AND WE REALLY SHOULD TOAST IN THE NEW YEAR WITH A LITTLE BUBBLY.
12-30
ARE YOU SURE? WATER'S FINE...
NO...
WOULD YOU PLEASE BRING US A BOTTLE OF YOUR BEST CARBONATED WATER?

HERE'S TO BLUE SKIES AND BETTER DAYS.
12-31
I HOPE I DON'T SCREW THIS UP!
I HOPE I DON'T SCREW THIS UP!
SPARKLING WATER

Resource Section

Does Someone You Care About Drink Too Much?

If you find yourself concerned about the drinking habits of a loved one—or even yourself—getting answers can be daunting. To cut through the confusion, it helps to understand the difference between *alcohol abuse* and *alcohol dependence*. Making this distinction can help you think clearly about a "drinking problem"— and allow you or a loved one to get the kind of help that makes a difference.

Alcohol dependence, often called *alcoholism*, is only one potential complication of drinking. Alcohol abuse can disrupt lives as well. In its diagnostic manual, the American Psychiatric Association defines alcohol abuse as drinking that leads to "clinically significant impairment or distress." For example:

- Neglecting major responsibilities at work, school, or home

- Drinking in hazardous situations, such as before driving
- Drinking that leads to recurrent legal problems, such as arrests for disorderly conduct
- Continued drinking even when it leads to recurrent social problems, such as violent arguments

Those consequences are serious enough. But alcohol dependence can involve any of them, and it goes on to include the following:

- Tolerance—drinking in greater quantities in order to achieve a desired level of intoxication.
- Withdrawal—feeling symptoms of illness when alcohol is not available. Examples of those symptoms are anxiety, nausea, vomiting, trembling, confusion, seizures, and hallucinations.
- Compulsive use—drinking that continues even after a person makes repeated promises to quit or experiences significant problems that relate directly to alcohol use.

In short, dependence has two dimensions. One is psychological: the belief that alcohol is essential to functioning in daily life. The other one is physiological: feeling extreme discomfort when access to alcohol is delayed or denied. Alcoholics Anonymous defines alcoholism simply as "a physical compulsion, coupled with a mental obsession to drink."

How Does Alcoholism Evolve?

A common scenario happens when a drinker moves from casual alcohol use to abuse and then to dependence. The difference is really a matter of degree. When drinkers start experiencing tolerance and withdrawal, they are at a point where they move into dependence.

Not all drinkers, however, follow a fixed path from abuse to dependence. Some remain abusers all their lives. And others cross the line to dependence soon after their first drink.

It's also important to remember that it's not the amount of alcohol consumed that defines the difference between abuse and dependence. Instead, the problem can be measured by the impact of drinking on somebody's life. The real question is, what's your—or your loved one's—level of impairment and distress?

Alcohol abusers may be more episodic in their problems, but they pose the same grave danger to themselves as well as the general public. If they're involved in an alcohol-related accident, a court may order them to undergo a chemical dependency assessment or attend substance abuse education classes. If they seek chemical dependency treatment, they generally find their way into an outpatient treatment program.

This may contrast with people who are dependent on alcohol, or those who cannot drink safely at all. The depth of their drinking problem may call for intensive inpatient treatment—a residential program that removes them from the people, places, and things associated with their alcohol use.

An alcohol-related diagnosis is complex. That's why it makes sense to turn to professional help when you have a concern about alcohol use. See your doctor and ask for a referral to someone trained in chemical dependency treatment. Getting an expert assessment up front can save time—and perhaps save your life. Several resources are listed on pages **131–133** to assist you in locating help.

How Can You Tell If Someone You Love Is an Alcoholic?

If you worry about someone's drinking, you're not alone. According to the most recent figures from the National Institute on Alcohol Abuse and Alcoholism

(NIAAA), 13.7 million U.S. adults meet the criteria for alcohol abuse or alcohol dependence. Still, people might struggle for years with the question, how can I tell if the person I love is truly an alcoholic?

Fortunately you don't have to be a medical professional to answer that question and take appropriate action. One simple option is to use a four-item questionnaire developed by Dr. John Ewing. The first letter of a key word in each question forms the acronym CAGE:

- Have you ever felt you should Cut down on your drinking?
- Have people Annoyed you by criticizing your drinking?
- Have you ever felt bad or Guilty about your drinking?
- Have you ever had a drink first thing in the morning to steady your nerves or to get rid of a hangover (Eye opener)?

You can pose these questions directly to your loved one, or come up with your own answers for that person. According to NIAAA, one "yes" answer signals a possible problem, and more than one means that it's time for your loved one to get help.

Another way to help determine if your loved one is an alcoholic is to learn about the way alcoholism is diagnosed. In the United States, professionals commonly use the criteria listed in the *Diagnostic and Statistical Manual of Mental Disorders* (DSM).

According to DSM criteria, people who are alcohol dependent (alcoholic) will do the following:

- Show tolerance (find that they have to drink more to get their desired effect from alcohol)
- Experience withdrawal symptoms when the effects of alcohol wear off
- Drink larger amounts over a longer period of time than intended
- Consistently fail to cut down or control their drinking
- Give up important work or personal activities in favor of drinking
- Spend a great deal of time getting alcohol, drinking it, and recovering from its effects
- Continue to drink despite knowledge of a persistent physical or psychological problem caused or exacerbated by drinking

To satisfy a diagnosis of alcohol dependence, a person must experience at least three of these criteria during a twelve-month period. People who are not alcohol dependent may still meet the criteria for alcohol abuse, a condition listed separately in the DSM. Alcohol abusers can limit the amount they drink when the consequences become severe enough. People who are truly dependent on alcohol cannot do this.

If you drink alcoholic beverages, you can find out
if your drinking habits are safe or harmful by taking a
confidential self-assessment at www.alcoholscreening.org.
This screening is sponsored by Join Together, a project at the
Boston University School of Public Health.

What Should You Say to Someone Who Drinks Too Much?

Alcoholics often deny that they have a drinking problem. Many will not seek help on their own. Left alone, these people often experience severe consequences of their drinking before getting help. Some literally drink themselves to death.

That's hard news if you're concerned about a friend or family member's drinking. But there's good news, too. By skillfully approaching this person, you can make a lifesaving difference.

Most people who decide to enter treatment for alcoholism claim that it was the influence of a close friend or loved one that actually helped them make the decision. According to a Gallup Poll, 94 percent of Americans believe it's their responsibility to intervene when a friend has a problem with alcohol or other drugs. But the poll also showed that only 38 percent feel "very confident and comfortable" in approaching that friend.

Using the following guidelines can help you gain the kind of influence needed to start a loved one on a path to recovery:

- **Time your message carefully.** Talk to a loved one shortly after he or she has experienced a problem related to drinking. These problems could range from a family argument to divorce, loss of a job, or an arrest for driving while intoxicated.
- **Avoid talking to someone while he or she is intoxicated.** Wait until the following day when the person is clear-headed and when the problem related to

drinking is still fresh in his or her mind. At that time, you have a better chance of getting your message across.

- **Focus on consequences.** It's usually best to talk to people about how their drinking is actually hurting them. Explain to your loved one how his or her drinking behavior is self-defeating. Focus on the discomfort, the psychological distress, and the emotional pain your loved one feels. You can say things like "It really hurts me to see you go through all of this."

- **Avoid lecturing.** Some people assume that a direct, hard-edged confrontation is the only way they can convince a loved one to get help. But this strategy often backfires. Sermonizing or scolding people for their behavior may invite further resistance and denial. Instead, take a compassionate approach and show care and respect for the individual. Use non-judgmental language and don't blame or criticize.

Don't label the person as an alcoholic or demand that he or she seek treatment. State your concerns and encourage your loved one to be assessed by an addiction professional.

- **Maintain rapport.** When approaching a loved one about a drinking problem, one of the most important things you can do is to maintain rapport. If you make a comment that this person interprets as shaming or blaming, you weaken that rapport.

- **Expect the worst.** Your loved one might get angry, deny the drinking problem, and tell you to mind your own business. Don't take it personally; these are common reactions. Denial is one of the unfortunate symptoms of alcoholism. After your loved one cools down and experiences more negative consequences from drinking, he or she might take your message to heart. You may have planted the seed for recovery.

- **Offer assistance in getting help.** If your friend is ready for help, be prepared to refer that person to a source of help, such as an Alcoholics Anonymous group or a treatment center. Escort him or her to the source of help and take part in the process as needed.

To find out more about getting help for alcoholism, resources can be found on pages **131–133** of this book.

What Is Alcoholics Anonymous?

American history includes many social movements that aimed to help people stop drinking. There was Prohibition, of course. But there was also the Anti-Saloon League, the American Temperance Society, the Washingtonian Temperance Society, the Woman's Christian Temperance Union, and more. Only one such movement survived: Alcoholics Anonymous (AA).

AA not only survived, it spread across the world. Today, AA lists its membership at 2,160,013, with 100,766 groups in Africa, Asia, and Europe as well as North and South America. If ever there was evidence that sobriety can be mass-produced, it is in AA.

AA began with the chance meeting of two people on May 12, 1935: Bill W., an alcoholic stockbroker from New York, and Bob S., an alcoholic surgeon in Akron, Ohio. Bill got sober through a set of principles that, he felt, had saved his life (ideas that later evolved into the Twelve Steps of AA). He shared those principles with Dr. Bob. Dr. Bob's "dry date" of June 10, 1935, is officially counted as AA's founding.

Bill and Dr. Bob began working with other alcoholics, helping them achieve sobriety one day at a time. And in 1939, the group published the book *Alcoholics Anonymous* to explain its Twelve Step program of recovery.

The only requirement for membership is a desire to stop drinking. There are no dues or fees for AA membership; AA is a self-supporting organization through its members' contributions. AA members engage in a set of activities suggested by the Twelve Steps, such as

- telling the truth—that they are addicted and cannot stop drinking on their own
- admitting and releasing resentments and fears
- making amends to people they've harmed
- engaging in prayer and meditation
- sharing AA principles with others who want to stop drinking

AA members describe their program as spiritual, not religious. No creed or ritual is required, and from the beginning, AA has welcomed atheists and agnostics. At the same time, members seek daily guidance from a Higher Power. That term is defined individually. For some members, it is the God of a church. Other members find their Higher Power in a friend, in nature, in the book *Alcoholics Anonymous,* in their AA group, or in many other sources of outside help.

To find an AA meeting near you, look in your local phone book under "alcoholism." Or, contact AA World Services at PO Box 459, New York, NY 10163, 212-870-3400.

How Does Al-Anon Work?

Alcoholism can touch every aspect of a family's life. Consider Brenda's story. She lost a father to alcoholism, and her brother developed the disease. She also married a problem drinker. They had a large family, and her husband left the job of parenting to her.

"I had out-of-control children at home," she says. "There was no structure—no rules, no bedtime schedules. It was just chaos." Brenda tried to structure the household but found that she couldn't do it alone. Some of her children developed behavior problems at school and eventually abused alcohol them-selves. For nearly a decade, Brenda searched for support. She went to parent meetings at school. She went to marriage counseling. She went to churches and Bible study groups. Finally, a therapist suggested Al-Anon.

"I remember listening to people at my very first Al-Anon meeting and think-ing, *This is where I belong,*" Brenda recalls. "The stories I was hearing there were about the very kinds of things happening in my life."

Al-Anon offers free and confidential support for anyone affected by an al-coholic or problem drinker. This includes parents, grandparents, spouses, part-ners, coworkers, and friends. Alateen, a part of Al-Anon, is a recovery program for young people impacted by a loved one's alcoholism.

Founded in 1951 by the wives of two Alcoholics Anonymous members, Al-Anon is based on AA's Twelve Steps. There are no dues and no fees. Rather than relying on mental health professionals, members lead self-help meetings in a spirit of mutual help. The purpose is to share their hope, strength, and experience in dealing with an alcoholic loved one.

It works. Today more than 24,000 Al-Anon groups exist in 115 countries.

Al-Anon begins with the principle that alcoholism is a family disease. And those who care most about the alcoholic are affected the most.

Al-Anon literature compares life with an alcoholic to a drama where people develop stereotypical, almost scripted, roles. Their behaviors center on the alcoholic and are dominated by the following characteristics:

- Obsession—going to great lengths to stop the alcoholic's drinking, such as searching the house for hidden stashes of liquor, secretly pouring drinks down the drain, or listening continually for the sound of opening beer cans.

- Anxiety—worrying constantly about the effects of the alcoholic's drinking on the children, the bills, and the family's future.

- Anger—feelings of resentment that result from being repeatedly deceived and hurt by the alcoholic.

- Denial—ignoring, making excuses for, or actively hiding the facts about the alcoholic's behavior.

- Guilt—family members' belief that they are somehow to blame for the alcoholic's behavior.

- Insanity—this is defined in Al-Anon as "doing the

same thing over and over and expecting different results."

With help from their peers, Al-Anon members learn an alternative: detachment with love. This happens when family members admit that they did not *cause* their loved one's alcoholism, nor can they *control* or *cure* it. Sanity returns to family life when members focus on taking care of themselves, changing the things that they can, and letting go of the rest.

As a result, alcoholic family members are no longer shielded from the consequences of their own behavior. This, more than anything else, can help them face the facts about their addiction and admit their need for help.

"Since I've been in Al-Anon, my life has totally changed," says Brenda. "I filed for divorce and set up my own household. Now my children are getting a lot more of their needs met with a lot more stability in their lives, and I'm a much happier parent. Since I moved out, my son has been on the honor roll at school and my daughter has had the best two years of her life."

To learn more about Al-Anon, call 757-563-1600 or go online to www.al-anon.alateen.org.

(Portions of the preceding information were originally published in Hazelden's *Alive and Free,* a health column that educates newspaper readers on the prevention and treatment of substance abuse issues. More *Alive and Free* articles and a full range of treatment-related resources can be found on the Hazelden Web site at www.hazelden.org.)

Helpful Organizations

Adult Children of Alcoholics (ACA)

PO Box 3216
Torrance, CA 90510
310-534-1815 (message only)
www.adultchildren.org

ACA is a Twelve Step, Twelve Tradition program of women and men who grew up in alcoholic or otherwise dysfunctional homes.

Al-Anon/Alateen

1600 Corporate Landing Parkway
Virginia Beach, VA 23454-5617
757-563-1600 (Main World Service Office number. Spanish available.)
www.al-anon.alateen.org

Alcoholics Anonymous (AA)

General Service Office
PO Box 459
New York, NY 10163
212-870-3400
www.alcoholics-anonymous.org

AA is a fellowship of men and women who share their experience, strength, and hope with each other so that they may solve their common problem and help others recover from alcoholism. The only requirement for membership is a desire to stop drinking. AA is not allied with any sect, denomination, political group, organization, or institution and does not wish to engage in any controversy. AA neither endorses nor opposes any causes. Members' primary purpose is to stay sober and help other alcoholics to achieve sobriety.

Cocaine Anonymous (CA)

3740 Overland Ave. Suite C
Los Angeles, CA 90034
or
PO Box 492000
Los Angeles, CA 90049-8000
310-559-5833
www.ca.org

CA is a Twelve Step recovery program concerned solely with the personal recovery and continued sobriety of individual drug addicts who turn to the Fellowship for help. CA does not engage in the fields of drug addiction research, medical or psychiatric treatment, drug education, or propaganda in any form—although members may participate in such activities as individuals.

Marijuana Anonymous (MA)

PO Box 2912
Van Nuys, CA 91404
800-766-6779
www.marijuana-anonymous.org

MA is a fellowship of men and women whose purpose is to stay free of marijuana. MA uses an adapted version of the Twelve Steps.

Nar-Anon Family Groups

22527 Crenshaw Blvd. #200B
Torrance, CA 90505
310-534-8188 or 800-477-6291
www.nar-anon.org

Nar-Anon is a Twelve Step program designed to help relatives and friends of drug addicts recover from the effects of living with an addicted relative or friend. Nar-Anon's program of recovery is adapted from Narcotics Anonymous.

Narcotics Anonymous (NA)

Main Office
PO Box 9999
Van Nuys, CA 91409
818-773-9999
www.na.org

NA is an international, community-based association of recovering drug addicts with more than 33,500 weekly meetings in more than 116 countries worldwide.

National Alliance on Mental Illness (NAMI)

Colonial Place Three
2107 Wilson Boulevard, Suite 300
Arlington, VA 22201-3042
703-524-7600 (main office)
703-516-7227 (TDD)
800-950-6264 (information helpline)
www.nami.org
www.nami.org/helpline

NAMI is a nonprofit, grassroots, self-help support and advocacy organization of families and friends of people with severe mental illnesses, such as schizophrenia, major depression, bipolar disorder, obsessive-compulsive disorder, and anxiety disorders.

National Suicide Prevention Lifeline

1-800-273-TALK (8255)
www.suicidepreventionlifeline.org

The National Suicide Prevention Lifeline is a national, twenty-four-hour, toll-free suicide prevention service available to all those seeking help in suicidal crisis. Callers will be routed to the closest possible provider of mental health and suicide prevention services.

Substance Abuse and Mental Health Services Administration (SAMHSA) National Clearinghouse for Alcohol and Drug Information (NCADI)

PO Box 2345
Rockville, MD 20847-2345
1-800-729-6686
www.ncadi.samhsa.gov

SAMHSA's National Clearinghouse for Alcohol and Drug Information (NCADI) is the nation's one-stop resource for information about substance abuse prevention and addiction treatment. SAMHSA is staffed by both English- and Spanish-speaking information specialists who are skilled at recommending appropriate publications, posters, and videos; conducting customized searches; providing grant and funding information; and referring people to appropriate organizations.

Recommended Reading

The following books discuss the basics of how alcoholism or drug addiction affect one's life and how to begin the recovery process. All books are published by Hazelden unless stated otherwise.

The Addictive Personality: Understanding the Addictive Process and Compulsive Behavior, by Craig Nakken

Addictive Thinking: Understanding Self-Deception, by Abraham J. Twerski, M.D.

Alcoholics Anonymous (The Big Book), published by Alcoholics Anonymous World Services, Inc.

Clean: A New Generation in Recovery Speaks Out, by Chris Beckman

Each Day a New Beginning: Daily Meditations for Women, by Karen Casey

First Year Sobriety: When All That Changes Is Everything, by Guy Kettelhack

A Gentle Path through the Twelve Steps: The Classic Guide for All People in the Process of Recovery, by Patrick Carnes, Ph.D.

Stop the Chaos: How to Get Control of Your Life by Beating Alcohol and Drugs, by Allen A. Tighe, M.S., C.C.D.C.R.

Twenty-Four Hours a Day

A Woman's Way through the Twelve Steps, by Stephanie S. Covington, Ph.D.

The following books discuss what family members can do when a loved one is an alcoholic or addicted to drugs.

Addict in the Family: Stories of Loss, Hope, and Recovery, by Beverly Conyers

Beyond Codependency: And Getting Better All the Time, by Melody Beattie

Codependent No More: How to Stop Controlling Others and Start Caring for Yourself, by Melody Beattie

Get Your Loved One Sober: Alternatives to Nagging, Pleading, and Threatening, by Robert J. Meyers, Ph.D., and Brenda L. Wolfe, Ph.D.

It Will Never Happen to Me: Growing Up with Addiction as Youngsters, Adolescents, Adults, by Claudia Black, Ph.D.

The Language of Letting Go, by Melody Beattie

Love First: A New Approach to Intervention for Alcoholism and Drug Addiction, by Jeff Jay and Debra Jay

More Language of Letting Go, by Melody Beattie

About the Author

Tom Batiuk is the creator of *Funky Winkerbean,* the celebrated comic strip distributed by King Features Syndicate to more than four hundred newspapers nationwide. Batiuk has created other strips as well. In 1979, he launched into syndication *John Darling,* the adventures of a fictional talk-show host. In 1987, he created his third comic strip, *Crankshaft,* which is based on an irascible school bus driver and appears in three hundred newspapers. Batiuk's strips have been collected in twenty-two full-length books. His focus on social issues like alcoholism, teen pregnancy, and breast cancer has put him at the forefront of comic art history. Over the years he has been honored with several awards including the Ohio Governor's Award, the Media Citation Award from the Journalism Education Association, and the Distinguished Service Award from the Music Educators National Conference. Batiuk and his wife live in Ohio.

Hazelden Foundation, a national nonprofit organization founded in 1949, helps people reclaim their lives from the disease of addiction. Built on decades of knowledge and experience, Hazelden's comprehensive approach to addiction addresses the full range of individual, family, and professional needs, including addiction treatment and continuing care services for youth and adults, publishing, research, higher learning, public education, and advocacy.

A life of recovery is lived "one day at a time." Hazelden publications, both educational and inspirational, support and strengthen lifelong recovery. In 1954, Hazelden published *Twenty-Four Hours a Day*, the first daily meditation book for recovering alcoholics, and Hazelden continues to publish works to inspire and guide individuals in treatment and recovery, and their loved ones. Professionals who work to prevent and treat addiction also turn to Hazelden for evidence-based curricula, informational materials, and videos for use in schools, treatment programs, and correctional programs.

Through published works, Hazelden extends the reach of hope, encouragement, help, and support to individuals, families, and communities affected by addiction and related issues.

For questions about Hazelden publications, please call 800-328-9000 or visit us online at hazelden.org/bookstore.

Other titles that may interest you, available from Hazelden:

Twenty-Four Hours a Day
This book helps readers develop a spiritual program, relate the Twelve Steps to their everyday lives, and accomplish their treatment and aftercare goals.
Softcover, 400 pp.   Order No. 5093

The Little Red Book
Filled with practical information for those first few days of sober living, this book is the original study guide to Alcoholics Anonymous.
Softcover, 160 pp.   Order No. 1034

Spilled Gravy
Ed Driscoll
Whether stirring the soul with his personal account of the tragedy of alcoholism, or celebrating the humor in everyday life, Driscoll's provocative memoir chronicles his rocky road to recovery and the hilarious hiccups along the way.
Softcover, 208 pp.   Order No. 2610

Denial Is Not a River in Egypt
Sandi Bachom, illustrated by Don Ross
This collection of fifty years of traditional AA slogans and quotations offers a wealth of insightful humor about denial.
Softcover, 104 pp.   Order No. 1638